CATALOGING PHONORECORDINGS
PROBLEMS AND POSSIBILITIES

PRACTICAL LIBRARY
AND INFORMATION SCIENCE

edited by

JAY E. DAILY

*Graduate School of Library
and Information Sciences
University of Pittsburgh
Pittsburgh, Pennsylvania*

Volume 1: Cataloging Phonorecordings: Problems and Possibilities,
Jay E. Daily

OTHER VOLUMES IN PREPARATION

CATALOGING PHONORECORDINGS

Problems and Possibilities

JAY E. DAILY

*Graduate School of Library
and Information Sciences
University of Pittsburgh
Pittsburgh, Pennsylvania*

MARCEL DEKKER, INC.   New York

MARCEL DEKKER, INC.

270 Madison Avenue, New York, New York 10016

LIBRARY OF CONGRESS CATALOG CARD NUMBER: 73-90723

ISBN: 0-8247-6196-0

Current printing (last digit):
10 9 8 7 6 5 4 3 2 1

PRINTED IN THE UNITED STATES OF AMERICA

Dedicated to the memory of Milton Cross, 1897–1975, The Metropolitan Opera of New York, and Texaco, who have furnished the author with a free musical education from the age of eight when on Christmas Day, 1931, he discovered a new and endlessly thrilling world.

CONTENTS

PREFACE

With so many competing authorities, each offering a method of cataloging phonorecordings that can be praised either for its adherence to tradition or its innovative properties, it might seem that another book would be unnecessary, especially in view of two alternatives of title unit entry provided in <u>Organization of Nonprint Materials</u> by the undersigned. Several years experience in the classroom has convinced most teachers that what students lack is not so much rigid rules of form as understanding of the problems involved, among which a lack of a standard and universally accepted authority is foremost. As the first section of the book explains, this is not meant to advocate a method of cataloging. It is offered as a means of understanding what the possibilities are. A knowledge of music is a definite advantage, and within limitations, the dedication of this book explains to whom the author is indebted for the little he knows. Beyond that the acknowledgments further explain the author's indebtedness.

All this is simply further proof that no one writes a book and prepares it for publication without the assistance of many other people, including the critics of earlier works. One point must be emphasized repeatedly. This book does not advocate the use of title main entry for anything. Main entry systems are used when only one entry contains full description of the work. All other entries are abbreviated in some way so that reference to the main entry is necessary for the user who wishes a full description. Considering the ease of card duplication, it is rather simpler mechanically to use a unit card system and reproduce full description for each point of access. It is apparent that this is essential for only the larger libraries of phonorecordings requiring immediate access through many different kinds of entries. It should not be too much to hope that no reader will be led to believe that an entry would not be made for composer just because title unit entry is used as a teaching device in this work. If unit cards are duplicated for all the entries possible, there would of course be entries for composers and performers as needed.

Most small libraries will find that brieflisting is adequate and efficient. In order to become skilled at this method of cataloging the student must be aware of what the essential elements of description are and how they can be listed to provide maximum access to the greatest number of users with minimum waste of time in searching. Very large libraries utilizing a computer will find that the unit entry system included here will provide for maximum access without requiring the cataloger to select among possible entries for the one that is somehow main without serving another purpose than coming at the head of the entry. Where all entries are of equal content, the question of main entry is at best an exercise in traditionalism and at worst the practice of futility.

At some later date, there will be rules of description using the punctuation of International Standard Bibliographic Description that adequately resolve many of these problems. The principal deficiency of Library of Congress cataloging is its blindness to the importance of the name of the performer in the identification of a phonorecording. To relegate the performer to level of a note is to miss the whole difference between printed music and its recorded performances. While this puts the author firmly on the other side of the "just-like-books" controversy, there seems to be no other position if any awareness is to be offered students who might find massive differences in appearance and utilization between books and phonorecordings.

These biases are explained here lest anyone say that the author is trying to pull a fast one by offering as standard what is, in fact, innovative. If this book had another purpose than an approach to learning how to catalog phonorecordings, if it were offered as a standard or an authority in the field, there would be little excuse for not attempting to find some comfortable middle ground that might not please everyone but would at least not annoy the average critic into a state of hysterical misapprehension. Until the compromises that are necessary to achieve universal bibliographic control reach the level of audiographic control, and even beyond that happy time, this book will still meet its intent if it provides those interested or required to learn what phonorecordings are all about with the confidence necessary to create records that will make access to a collection fit the user's needs and abilities.

This is the first of a series of books meant to provide a practical approach to the problems of technical service librarians and their assistants. Several titles are projected for this series with authors who have devoted years to consideration of the problems involved. A preface is scarcely the place for promises, but the aspiration of the author who is also the editor of the series is to develop an approach to theory by solid investigation of what is practical and applicable. This seems to be the only way to make the vast increase of information sources a boon rather than the bane of anyone's existence, least of all catalogers. We are, it seems, rather like Samuel Johnson's definition of a lexicographer: harmless drudges who make catalogs. The object is to make them usable without wasted effort, and toward this high purpose this book is the first thrust.

Jay E. Daily
Pittsburgh, Pennsylvania

ACKNOWLEDGMENTS

The author is deeply indebted to his colleagues, Ms. Patricia Oyler, Dr. Martha Manheimer, and Mr. George Sinkankas, for many helpful suggestions and the willingness to listen to theorizing at all hours. Though not directly involved, Ms. Mildred Myers greatly influenced the author, so that anything of value is the happy result of previous collaboration. Ms. Darlene Fawcett, Ms. Barbara Wonders, and Ms. Jo Ann Hartz prepared the manuscript with such competence and thoroughness that the author cannot sufficiently praise their work, and Mr. Grant Lee read the manuscript for errors of stylistic omission and commission.

The author must thank his students at the Graduate School of Library and Information Sciences who have taught him to respect the problems of cataloging phonorecordings enough that an explanation in detail is possible. The author is also indebted to Ms. Ruth Weisberg, Librarian of Station WQED in Pittsburgh, whom he has the honor to serve as consultant, for assistance she might not recognize that evolved from many enjoyable conversations. The author's wife tolerated the disarray that such work incurs without a murmur, and when energies flagged provided as always encouragement, sustenance, and the happiest of environments.

HOW TO USE THIS BOOK

There are no standardized methods for cataloging phonorecordings, and such rules as exist are often of local application only. Soon after the <u>Anglo-American Cataloging Rules</u> were published in 1967, the deficiency of the section devoted to phonorecordings was noted in the professional literature. The Library of Congress prepares cards for some phonorecordings, generally following the <u>Anglo-American Cataloging Rules</u>, hence suffering from the deficiencies found in the rules themselves. First, all entries are under composer, or composer-equivalent , or title, a procedure that delays the cataloging of all but serious, or classical, music. Second, provisions for main-entry cataloging are assumed to be applicable to unit-entry cataloging, when this is manifestly unnecessary and a complication not needed in the unit-entry system. Finally, subject headings duplicate a uniform title by combining form of composition with medium of performance.

The unit entry system allows for entries of equal value for whatever may be considered important by the individual library. It is equally applicable for a computerized and for a manual system. In a manual system, the assumption is made that the cards will be duplicated by any of the common methods: xerography, offset reproduction, mimeograph, or automated typewriter. Entries are added for each of the cards so duplicated and they are filed in alphabetic order. The result is complete cataloging under each entry with minimum effort. A library that must provide access to all the performers as well as composers will find that this method of cataloging is particularly efficient. Its obvious disadvantage is that a great number of cards are produced and must be filed.

The problem for the library technical assistant who wants to learn how to catalog phonorecordings is especially difficult. If he learns one system, can he adapt his knowledge to another? The answer is obvious: only if the system he learns incorporates all others. Like the magpie's nest in the fable, unit-entry cataloging for a music research library

encompasses all possible variations. Furthermore, it provides in-
sight into the nature of commercially available phonorecordings, so
that a cataloger who understands computerized or manual unit-entry
cataloging can adapt his knowledge to whatever system he finds in a
library. When a library finds that it is providing too little access for
its patrons, the unit-entry system will be found most useful, ultimately,
although obviously considerably more elaborate than any but the main-
entry system established through use of the Anglo-American Cataloging
Rules. Even for the main-entry system, the knowledge of unit-entry
cataloging is essential. The order of elements in a catalog entry is
of primary importance, and the chief work of learning to catalog must
be devoted to an identification of the elements.

This book is devoted to a full explanation with examples of the unit-
entry system. The first two chapters explain the essentials of those
elements that also constitute a means of identifying the contents of a
phonorecording; the third chapter explains the elements that identify
the phonorecording itself, rather than the contents; and the four
succeeding chapters are devoted to the analysis of the contents whether
individual works in a collection or characteristics of performance.
Very many examples are provided, each limited to matter already
explained, so that the progression of the learning process is not confused with unexplained exemplary material.

A chapter is then devoted to Library of Congress Cataloging and a
final chapter is devoted to examples and the development of brief-
form catalog entries, mentioned several places in previous chapters.
From this chapter the persistent student should be able to derive information that will serve him regardless of what he might find as the
standard method within a library. He should further be able to change
his method of cataloging if the library decides that its rules are inadequate or that it must add phonorecordings to its computerized cataloging
system. Brief-form cataloging is actually a method of preparing lists
from the unit entry to provide the user of a library with a means of
access that fits his inquiry. If he knows the composer and the work,
the list under composer will give him the phonorecording he desires.
If he is interested in the performer, he will find the list of performers
suitable for his needs. If he wants a particular work and knows the
conventional title, the list of fully analyzed phonorecordings will serve
him best. All the examples noted in the first chapters are fully developed in the last chapters.

If, as may well be the case, International Standard Bibliographic
Description is adopted for phonorecordings, the unit entries exemplified in this book will need no further reshaping to fit standards that

are derived from book cataloging. It is only a matter of punctuation,
easily learned, rather than a complete recording of the elements of
identification, as the following example shows. (Present Library of
Congress Cataloging is not comparable.)

Unit entry as International Standard Bibliographic Description:
    Symphony in A minor, no. 3. , Op. 56= Scotch /Felix
      Mendelssohn. -[Perf. by]/ Otto Klemperer cond. / The Phil-
      harmonia Orchestra. - Angel 35880. 12" LPM. - Contents:-
      Side 1, Bd. 1, = Overture = The Hebrides = Fingal's Cave,
      Op. 26.

Unit entry:
    Symphony in A minor, no. 3, Op. 56, "Scotch," by Felix
      Mendelssohn. Perf. by Otto Klemperer cond. The Philharmonia
      Orchestra. Angel 35880.
      12" LPM
      Contents:- Side 1, Bd. 1, Overture "The Hebrides" (Fingal's
      Cave), Op. 26.

For this example the following entries would be required:

    Mendelssohn, Felix, 1809-1847.
      Symphony in A minor, no. 3, Op. 56, "Scotch," by Felix
      Mendelssohn. Perf. by Otto Klemperer cond. The Philharmonia
      Orchestra. Angel 35880.
      12" LPM
      Contents:- Side 1, Bd. 1, Overture "The Hebrides" (Fingal's
      Cave), Op. 26.

    "Scotch"
      Symphony in A minor, no. 3, Op. 56, "Scotch," by Felix....

    Overture "The Hebrides" (Fingal's Cave), Op. 26. +
      [Symphony in A minor, no. 3, Op. 56, "Scotch," by Felix....

    "The Hebrides" (Fingal's Cave), Op. 26. +
      [Symphony in A minor, no. 3, Op. 56, "Scotch," by Felix....

    "Fingal's Cave" (The Hebrides), Op. 26. +
      [Symphony in A minor, no. 3, Op. 56, "Scotch," by Felix....

    Klemperer, Otto, cond. The Philharmonia Orchestra
      [Symphony in A minor, no. 3, Op. 56, "Scotch," by Felix....

    The Philharmonia Orchestra cond. by Otto Klemperer
      [Symphony in A minor, no. 3, Op. 56, "Scotch," by Felix....

Whether the punctuation of International Standard Bibliographic Description or that shown as unit entry is employed, the rules for the creation of entries are remarkably simple and mechanistic. An entry is made for anything in quotation marks, anything following the word "by," anything following the words "Perf. by," and for anything in the section beginning with the word "Contents."

Brief-form cataloging relies on a single entry taking the most important element first. In the usual library with a collection of serious music, this will be the composer, so that the unit entry shown above would yield the following entry in abbreviated cataloging as compared with brief form.

Abbreviated entry:
    Mendelssohn: Symphony in A minor, no. 3, "Scotch." Angel
       35880. 12" LPM. With Overture "The Hebrides" (Fingal's
       Cave) Side 1, Bd. 1.

Brief-form entry:
    Mendelssohn: Symphony no. 3, "Scotch." Angel 35880.

In those libraries where the performer is most important and brief-form cataloging is essential, the inclusion of the performer is simply a matter of rearranging the elements:

    Klemperer: Mendelssohn, Symphony in A minor, no. 3, "Scotch."
       Angel 35880. 12" LPM. With Overture "The Hebrides"
       (Fingal's Cave) Side 1, Bd. 1.

Anglo-American Cataloging Rules are briefly summarized in Chapter 6 for further study and practice work. Fully developed rules with examples are much more meaningful after an understanding of phonorecordings has already been acquired.

The only essential reference tool for the cataloger is <u>Schwann Record and Tape Guide</u>, which is both an excellent and reliable source of information and a very inexpensive amanuensis. With all the explanation and examples, however, no claim is made that this book will supplant actual experience. To understand how to catalog phonorecordings, practice is essential, and no explanation, no matter how elaborate, can take the place of sitting down with a collection of phonorecordings and preparing a unit-entry catalog. The closest approximation is the duplication of information from the label of the phonorecording and the jacket, if necessary. The individual who wishes to catalog phonorecordings can claim to know how to do it only after he has had sufficient guided practice at the work.

CATALOGING PHONORECORDINGS
PROBLEMS AND POSSIBILITIES

Chapter 1

WRITTEN ON THE WIND

For nearly a century, since 1877, methods have existed for capturing
sounds and reproducing them. Thomas A. Edison, in his Camden
laboratory, first with tinfoil cylinders, then with an easily-molded
tarry substance, started not only an industry but a whole series of
inventions leading to the quick, inexpensive, and all but universal
methods of making and using phonorecordings today. The first ones
reproduced sounds mechanically using a large horn to give an approximation of the original sound made. The first commercially produced
phonorecordings were sold in velvet-lined boxes, because they were
very fragile cylinders. Museums and private collectors have kept
examples of these early recordings, and when they are played, we can
hear voices long dead singing songs long since forgotten.

One of the first improvements was making the cylinder into a round
disc, the first phonodisc. These were much easier to store and somewhat less subject to damage. Soon, even Edison's company saw the
advantage of discs, and very many famous people joined in the production of phonorecordings of all kinds. Even though nearly fifty years
passed before electrical recordings of sounds was developed, the
legendary voices of the past can still be heard, and after 1925, the
exact quality of voice fairly well judged. Caruso, who died in 1921,
is a legend that anyone can investigate by listening to his great tenor
voice, although the timbre is lost because of the mechanical method of
recording his operatic artistry. Another legendary voice, that of
Claudia Muzio, who died in 1936, can be reproduced so that it is
virtually identical with what was the living sound. Musicians have
greatly gained from listening to the way famous artists of the past
accomplished performances that are part of music history. Most
people who are interested in music have heard of Caruso, but rather
fewer know who Claudia Muzio was and why she was called the greatest
soprano of all time.

Phonodiscs were blank on one side, at one time, and then a way was found not only for putting recordings on both sides but also for arranging the grooves so that much more could be contained. A phonorecording of an opera or lengthy symphony would have required ten to twenty discs before 1948. Since the development of the long-playing phonorecording, and especially since stereophonic recording and reproduction became possible, the sounds are the same when made and when played, or so nearly so as makes little difference.

Phonotapes began as recordings on wire when it was discovered that magnetism could be used as a means of capturing sound. When these wires were flattened and attached as a thin coating to plastic strips, the cost of making such recordings was greatly reduced, and the most recent development puts the plastic tape into a container so that it is much less likely to unwind and is much easier to play. When the old wire recordings came off the spool, as they did readily, it was a time-consuming task to rewind the wire without damaging the recording. Now reel-to-reel tapes are becoming much less popular because cassettes and cartridges are more convenient and the quality of sound is equally good. A very recent development puts four tracks onto one cassette or cartridge so that four slightly different sounds come out of loudspeakers. The effect is supposed to be very like sitting in the ideal seat in a concert hall listening to music all around you.

Librarians soon realized that phonorecordings were valuable means of storing and retrieving information, and even before electrical recording was developed, some libraries were including collections of phonodiscs in their holdings. These were circulated like books by the most progressive libraries. Since that time, there has been less and less discussion of whether a library should include phonorecordings in its collection, although the argument raged in the library profession for a considerable length of time. Obviously a special music library relies heavily on phonorecordings as a significant part of its collection. Public libraries now circulate phonorecordings, in part because their patrons demand the service. School libraries, college and university libraries, and several kinds of special libraries included phonorecordings even before cassettes and cartridges were developed and made available through commercial sources. The sale of phonorecordings, however, is greatest to people who have home libraries.

The industry that has grown since Edison's invention is now worldwide, and parallels the book industry. Phonorecordings are produced, promoted, reviewed, and discussed like books. They may go out of print or may appear in re-recordings. There is even a service fulfilling a function for phonorecordings much like the trade bibliographies

that keep librarians abreast of publications in printed form. The
Schwann Record and Tape Guide and the Harrison Tape Catalog are the
standard tools of the commercial phonorecording industry. The
Library of Congress produces printed cards for phonorecordings, as
for books.

Nevertheless, the cataloging of phonorecordings is scarcely standardized, so that each library tends to develop its own rules if it does not
use Library of Congress cards. These have been found rather less
than adequate for most libraries because of the difficulty of locating
the card for a phonorecording, the delays in cataloging, and the limi-
tation to phonorecordings that the Library of Congress acquires. The
situation has become further confused by the necessity for libraries to
catalog whatever is locally made. With the improvement in techniques
of recording and of reproducing sound has come the increased possibility
that every library or institution can be its own producer of phonorecordings, for which no cataloging service out side the library is ever
available.

A further difficulty is found in the rules for cataloging based on the
experience of previous decades. Although the Library of Congress
follows the Anglo-American Cataloging Rules of 1967, these were the
subject of criticism soon after they were published, and most music
libraries find them woefully inadequate. With the development of
computerized methods in many large university libraries, the problem
has been compounded. The computer is capable of solving one of the
most vexing problems in the cataloging of phonorecording: there are
many more entries needed than is the case with the ordinary book. A
recording of an opera, to take the extreme example, would require
entries for the composer, the conductor, the principal singers, the
opera company, and possibly the librettists and related works, as well
as the title of the opera. Libraries have varied greatly in the number
and kind of entries made, from the bare essential of title and composer
to the fullest description. The computer is able to reach into an entry
and make lists according to the needs of the patrons. Until this rather
simple fact was completely understood, it seemed that the cataloging
of phonorecordings would always be the work of a highly skilled professional librarian.

Fortunately, that is not the case if the principles are explained and
understood. Although there is a tremendous variety of phonorecordings
in libraries, and the cataloging has ranged from minimum to maximum,
the whole subject can be brought into focus. A method can be established so that whatever a given library decides is the extent of cataloging
needed, the library technical assistant can prepare entries for a card

file or a computerized system that will meet the general requirement
of providing access to the informational content of the phonorecording
with ease on the part of the user and least effort on the part of the
cataloger. As is the case with books, the value of a collection is in
its use, and the use is determined by a knowledge of the contents.

KINDS OF CONTAINERS

The library is responsible for making the contents of a phonorecording
known and preserving the container. Although modern techniques make
the discs and tapes less subject to damage, they can be destroyed.
Even an "unbreakable" record will break if mistreated. A very large
collection of phonorecordings may have examples of all the different
methods used, possibly excepting Edison's original cylinders. These
are standardized, but they may not be interchangeable so far as equipment is concerned. The term phonorecording is used for all the
different kinds, although the common term is "record." But this is
too ambiguous to use in a library which may have different kinds of
records, including acquisitions files and archives. There are two
major classes of phonorecordings: phonodiscs and phonotapes.

Phonodiscs

The size may vary from seven inches to sixteen inches, and the speed
of the turntable for reproduction from 78 RPM to 16 2/3 RPM. The
common sizes are twelve-inch long-playing (33 1/3 RPM) and seven-
inch (45 RPM). The grooves on phonodiscs used for tracking the stylus
may be stereophonic, monophonic, or monaural, and even quadraphonic,
a very recent development. In quadraphonic recording two channels
are coded on each side of the groove so that four different amplifiers
can pick up the sound for four loudspeakers. Only time will decide
whether this will be as popular as stereophonic recordings.

Phonotapes

There are three kinds of packaging of phonotapes. Although the size
of the tape may vary, especially for professional recording equipment,
in reel-to-reel tapes quarter-inch is common enough to be considered
standard. This same size tape is used in cartridges which are 5 1/2
by 4 inches, approximately. The cartridges were supposed to be the
successor of phonodiscs because they are nearly indestructible and

provide sound of a very high quality. They can be played on compact equipment, even in a car, and the most recent development is quadraphonic cartridges. These are not compatible with the stereophonic cartridges and require special equipment.

Cassettes are even smaller than cartridges. In the plastic container provided with many kinds of cassettes, the measurement is 7 cm by 11 cm. At the thickest point, the cassette is only a half-inch, and in its container, the entire cassette is only 4 1/4 by 2 3/4 by 9/16. The quality of sound varies greatly with the type of tape used, and cassettes have proved to be much more subject to damage than cartridges. The tape may pull off the spool, or static electricity may cause it to wind onto the posts in the cassette player. A person with some manual dexterity and patience can unwind the tape and restore it to proper working order. The cassettes can be opened and tape can be replaced on the spool, even though the tape is only 1/8 inch wide.

Standard equipment for professional recording is still the reel-to-reel tape, and the length of the tape is the only variant. Quadraphonic tapes may be made on equipment no more expensive than the old monaural devices. The number of tracks is less often a variant than the speed at which the tape moves past the recording head or playback head.

The fastest speed, usually not available except on professional equipment, is 15 inches per second (ips) or 38 cm per second. Most tape decks include 7 1/2, 3 3/4, and 1 7/8 ips speed. The quality of sound decreases as the speed is reduced. The fastest speed is used for professional equipment because it has the greatest range, but only a very sophisticated instrument can detect the differences between 15 ips (38 cps) and 7 1/2 (19 cps), and for almost every kind of music the one is as good as the other. At slower speeds, however, reproduction quality fades, so that the slowest speed, 1 7/8 ips (4.75 cps), is suitable only for the speaking voice.

Reels are generally five inches or seven inches in diameter, especially if commercially produced recordings are in this form, regardless of the length of the tape. This may be as high as 3600 feet for a seven-inch reel. As with cassettes, the thinner the plastic tape on which the ferrite coating is placed, the more likely damage will occur. Half the length, 1800 feet, is thought to be sufficient for a reel. The length of cartridges is standard, but cassettes vary from 15 minutes total playing time to 120 minutes, with one hour of playing time on each side.

There are other means of recording music or voices, from piano

rolls to dictating machine belts, but these represent no problem to the
cataloger, except in describing the contents. In fact, granting the
compatibility of the equipment for the kind of phonorecordings in the
collection, each of the kinds is valuable in its own way and each has
disadvantages. Cassettes are so small that they are easily lost and
may be stolen by predatory users of the library. Cartridges seem to
have a questionable future, and the companies now producing them may
not do so in the years to come. Reel-to-reel tapes and equipment are
being taken off the market because cassettes are so much handier and
not nearly so expensive for tapes or equipment. The history of recorded sound has always been a story of one improvement crowding out
an old method. The real problem in cataloging is the contents.

WHAT IS CONTAINED

The first fact to keep in mind about phonorecordings is that a performer is always involved, and the question in cataloging is whether
the work performed or the performer is the reason for making the
phonorecording. There is as great a variety of phonorecordings as
there are different kinds of books, and with the development of the
cassette-tape recording devices, everyone can be his own producer.
The object of cataloging is to organize material so that it can readily
be found, and the organization must be at the level of the user. The
same method for cataloging phonorecordings in the music libraries of
universities is recommended and desirable, but elementary schools
or small public libraries need not provide as much detail nor as many
points of access to the collection.

An entry in a catalog is a point of access. The reason the computer
resolves many of the problems of cataloging phonorecordings is that
points of access are not dependent on entries. In a manual system, the
first line of the card determines how it will be filed in the card catalog.
This entry is really not dependent on the description of the work cataloged. When we identify a particular phonorecording, we must
distinguish it from all others. Providing access to the information on
the phonorecording means that we must make entries for all that the
users expect to find. These entries vary not only with the kind of
library for which the cataloging is done, but also for the kind of phonorecording that is being cataloged.

The tangle is not so impenetrable as may appear. Anything complex
can be sorted out into component parts so that when all the parts are

understood the whole is understandable and quite simple. With
phonorecordings, the first step is in sorting out phonorecordings by
the significance of the performers, because in that way we will auto-
matically be dealing with the chief difference between phonorecordings
and books. The Schwann Record and Tape Guide is in two separate
parts, one for music including current popular music and jazz, and the
other for spoken records and miscellaneous phonorecordings. This
will be our chief tool in untangling phonorecordings, and the methods
we suggest will be such that the tool will be useful to cataloger and
user alike. In fact, a home library of phonorecordings can be made
using the method of entry employed by the Schwann catalog. In reading
this book the beginning cataloger of phonorecordings should keep a
recent copy of the Schwann catalog at hand for ready reference. It is
not only a great aid to understanding, but it develops a very useful
habit.

Classical Music

A musicologist would consider the word "classical" to refer to the
period before the Romantic composers of the nineteenth century. This
term, however, has a certain popularity but is better than such terms
as "serious music" or "long-hair music," especially since popular
musicians began the style of wearing long hair. We might say this is
"enduring music" if not permanent music, because some compositions
were written several hundred years ago. If we accept the idea that
this kind of music has provided us with the classics, then classical
music is not such a bad term, although ambiguous. The term "serious
music" will be preferred throughout this book.

The Schwann catalog includes all the phonorecordings of this kind in
a "composer section." The distinction is valid, because the composer
and the performer share importance with the particular work. Some
performers become greatly skilled at playing music by a single composer, for instance Bach, Beethoven, or Chopin, and the collector of
phonorecordings is likely to want different interpretations of a certain
work. Performances can become very well known and may be recorded
and re-recorded, even if initially the purpose was to broadcast the
music over the radio. Arturo Toscanini, for instance, was considered
one of the greatest of all conductors, and some of his performances
broadcast in the period just before and just after the Second World War
are still available on phonorecordings.

If a collection of phonorecordings is limited to the music of great
composers, it can be cataloged in a fashion that closely resembles the

cataloging of books. This is very rarely the case, because much music is included in phonorecordings entered under the section "Collections, Classical" in the Schwann Record and Tape Guide. These cannot be treated "just like books" because they are vastly different. Some collections feature a performer, some feature a group of musicians, and some feature short pieces from one or several composers. Sometimes the collection has a title indicating the nature of the phonorecording, sometimes the title is rather humorous: "Verdi's Greatest Hits." A frequent problem for the cataloger is how to treat phonorecordings so that a performer who gives his name to the whole collection can be found with other works in which he has been included.

A further difficulty with classical music is that the work may lack a distinctive title and the form of composition be made to serve instead. Furthermore, the title given the work by the composer has about equal chance of surviving as titles given by musicologists and the general public. Beethoven called his third symphony "Eroica," a name that everyone accepts, but he never entitled his sonata "Moonlight," although that is the name that the music acquired. The "conventional title" and the title according to the form of the work have been used to identify compositions by well known composers but with several unnecessary difficulties. A collection of phonorecordings always requires many entries, and the solution is found in the unit-entry system, which separates the description of a work from the entries under which it can be found.

Popular Music

In collections of popular songs, the performer is much more important to the listener than the composer of the song. Until recently very little attention was paid to the composers of popular music. Not infrequently the composer is also the performer, and the title of the phonorecording may not indicate that this is the case. Some performers seem to be almost always in demand; others have a very short period of popularity. At one time, and in some places even today, libraries would exclude popular music on the basis that it is too insignificant to bother with. Actually, composers of serious music have often used folk songs and popular melodies in their compositions, and equally, a considerable amount of popular music is derived from the works of serious composers, usually long dead to avoid copyright restrictions. (When the composers of the once popular song "Avalon" were brought into court because the original melody was written by Giacomo Puccini as a tenor aria for the third act of Tosca, copyrighted by the Italian firm of Ricordi, one of them is supposed to have said, "How did I know it was copyrighted? I thought you had to be dead to write one of those things.")

Folk music, and country and western music, may lack an identifiable composer. One definition of folk music is that the composer cannot be determined. The cataloger may dislike one type of music or another, but he should be able to catalog all kinds with equal ability. The question of whether the library should collect one kind or another of the phonorecordings available has to be decided by the library director or the library's board of trustees or a committee of the faculty. A method of cataloging that makes including different kinds of phono-recordings impossible is a very poor way to organize any collection, whatever its rules of selection may be.

Jazz

As the only completely American contribution to musical history jazz requires special treatment. In serious music, playing a melody with such ornamentation as the performer wishes to include is called im-provisation. Jazz is played by a group of musicians, who may or may not be able to read music, exploring the possibilities of the work they are playing to demonstrate the use of the instrument each musician plays. It is truly a remarkable accomplishment.

Most jazz musicians are quite incapable of performing the same work twice in the same way. The date of the performance becomes as critical as the title of the composition in identifying the phonorecording. Sometimes the title of the composition is of significance only in identifying a particular performance.

The works of jazz musicians tend to be collected over a whole range of time, and a great performer never loses popularity with those who enjoy jazz. The phonorecordings that have gone out of circulation or are no longer commercially available may be sought avidly by a jazz enthusiast. Often these phonorecordings are re-recorded and re-issued under different labels and with a different title, creating a particular problem for the cataloger.

As a field of interest, jazz has attracted many important writers and served as the basis for much modern music, from Gershwin to Poulenc. A research library on music would include jazz because of its significance in the history of music and because of its influence on modern composers.

Spoken Records

Although the term "records" is very ambiguous, limited to phono-recordings of the human voice, it serves to distinguish an important and numerous class of library items in a collection of recorded sound. Libraries for the blind especially rely on the phonorecordings of readings. At one time these were made on sixteen-inch discs that were played at 16 2/3 ips, but the development of cassette tape recorders has eliminated almost all of the difficulty of making phonorecordings for the blind. Obviously the cataloging of this material serves the sighted librarian rather than the sightless patron, but the same rules apply as for cataloging other material, even though the material cataloged is a phonorecording of a book read aloud by a volunteer.

Foreign Languages

Similarly, changes in the methods of teaching foreign languages have greatly increased the number of phonorecordings for this instructional purpose. There are some companies that produce nothing but phono-recordings of basic language instruction with accompanying booklets. Linguists were able to show that a language is most readily learned if the process of learning the mother tongue is followed as closely as possible. In many institutions of education where languages are taught there are laboratories where the student can listen to the sounds of a language and reproduce them and then listen to his own voice and compare it with that of the native speaker of the language. This is highly effective as a method of instruction, and it depends entirely on the availability of inexpensive phonorecording equipment.

Instructional phonorecordings may include pep talks for salesmen, sound advice in spoken form for those who are engaged in some course of personal improvement, phonorecordings meant to be played with the listener learning in his sleep, and many other kinds of learning tools. It has been found that individuals may not learn as well by reading as they will by hearing words, and aside from the blind, there are phono-recordings for the training of animals - or possibly the training of their masters.

Very early in the history of phonorecordings, the performances of great actors were captured and much interest centered on the way poets read their own poems. Now many great plays are available in recorded form, in English and in foreign languages. There are phonorecordings of poetry read by well known actors, sometimes featuring the actor, sometimes featuring the poet.

All these kinds of phonorecordings can be cataloged by the same method as that used for music, with the assurance that at least one card will serve the user of a manual system by supplying information regardless of his method of searching for it. Whether the user looks for the author of a play, its title, or the actors who perform it, the card system should supply the identifying details. In a computerized system, the same result is achieved with or without the use of lists, book catalogs, or on-line inquiry using some form of computer console. There is a kind of phonorecording, however, in which nothing matters but the sound itself.

Sound Effects

Phonorecordings have been made of almost everything that is "written on the wind." There are phonorecordings of animal sound; bird song, the splashing of waves, and the laughter of people. This kind of phono-recording is useful only for the phenomena recorded, and such a collection could be organized much like a collection of pictures, using only subject headings to provide access to the phonorecordings.

Often such phonorecordings are used to demonstrate some kind of narration, and if this is the case, then the phonorecording should fit into a collection that includes material of all kinds. When this is the decision, then the methods explained in the subsequent chapters can be used for phonorecordings of sound effects, especially when accompanied by narration, but no effort will be made to explain how to catalog solely by subject access.

CONCLUSION

As can be seen from this review of the great variety of phonorecord-ings, the first question to be resolved is "what kind of phonorecording is this?" Organizing a collection of phonorecordings becomes fairly simple, once the depth of the analysis is determined and the identifying features of a phonorecording are separated from the points of access, those entries that the user needs to match his own information and to provide him with the exact location of the phonorecording he wishes to listen to.

The key question is: "Will the performer (or performers) require an entry?" For much serious music, all popular music and jazz, and many of the spoken records, the performer is highly significant.

Determining the role of the performer in the phonorecording will help
in categorizing the phonorecording. Once this is done, the choice of
appropriate uniform title and subject heading is generally easy. For
instance, in a phonorecording of a book read aloud for sightless users
of a library, the volunteer who has done the reading is due gratitude
but no attention in the catalog entry. It is much better to write a
letter thanking the reader than to include his name in describing the
phonorecording. In this case, the important thing is the title and
author of the book, just as if it were in print rather than on tape. A
phonorecording of a famous actor reading a book of poetry is another
matter entirely.

In the subsequent chapters the method of cataloging will show what
is the most complete entry that can be made and explain how entries
can be shortened to minimum detail for libraries that need no more
than that for their patrons. In order to create a brief listing, the
cataloger needs to know what to leave out. Because some information
is always omitted, this is not so simple a decision as it may appear,
especially if the difficulties of ascertaining the title of the phonorecording are taken into account.

Chapter 2

PRINCIPLES OF DESCRIPTION

   The first decision to be made after the phonorecording is examined is
where to find the label to be used in creating a catalog entry. Phonodiscs are sold in cardboard envelopes sometimes called a "record sleeve"
and sometimes, as here, referred to as the "phonodisc jacket" or just
"jacket." The company that produced the phonorecording may use the
phonodisc jacket for advertising the contents. There is an attention-
getting picture on one side and notes on the other. At the least the
title of the work (or works) and the names of the composer and of the
performer will be given along with an album number and the name of the
company. It might seem that this is an ideal source of information,
as indeed it is, except that the label does not always match the jacket.
Because one must have priority over the other, all information is taken
from the label on the phonodisc rather than from the jacket or other
sources. The information on the jacket may be included, if necessary,
but only as second choice.

   The reason for this rule is that jackets wear out in time and may not
be worth preserving. The label on the phonorecording is much more
permanent and should be replaced if it is damaged in any way. Phonotapes produced commercially will include a label on the reel, cartridge,
or cassette, as well as information on the box or on a detachable paper
included in the container. Locally produced phonorecordings should be
labeled as carefully as commercially produced examples. Whatever
becomes of the container, whether a box or a jacket, the phonorecording itself can be readily identified.

   If information is needed to complete the description of the phonorecording, it can be taken from the container, but this must be noted on the
catalog entry. The information that is found is sorted into a sequence
very like the catalog entry for a book. In computerized systems,
these portions of the catalog entry are called fields, and this makes a

useful way of thinking of the kinds of information to be included and the
order in which the information should be arranged. Even if a card for
a card catalog is prepared, the information should follow in the sequence
given. All variables in cataloging are noted, but because the sequence
is not a variable omitted information represents an omitted field rather
than a different field. This decision is necessary if there is to be any
standardization of entries in catalogs.

In the subsequent sections of this chapter the contents of each field
are elaborated with some detail. The remainder of this book takes
up each field and describes all the problems that may be encountered.
Even so, no rule of description can foretell what might occur. When
a difficulty of description arises, a professional librarian can be
consulted. However, with experience and, even more important, a
firm understanding of the principles of cataloging, a technical assistant
can resolve a problem. Usually the difficulty is a minor one, really,
and the great worry is why the item at hand does not conform with an
established and readily handled pattern. However, just as Vergil did
not write the <u>Aeneid</u> for twentieth-century students to translate,
phonorecording companies do not produce labels with the cataloger in
mind. So long as there is sufficient information to identify the item,
it can be cataloged. Where information is lacking, it can be supplied
if necessary, and omitted if unnecessary.

There are ten fields of information. In a computerized system these
fields are either searchable, that is, the computer can locate specific
items within a field, or they are unsearchable, so that the information
will be produced only if other information or the complete entry is
sought. In a manual system, the searchable fields indicate what
additional entries should be made so that individual names and subjects
can serve as points of access in a card catalog or a part of the index-
ing of a book catalog. In cataloging books, tracings are made to show
the additional entries included in the files of cards. However, in
cataloging phonorecordings, it is possible to create rules by which all
the entries can be located on the basis of what is included in the
"searchable" fields. The fields all serve as means of identifying a
phonorecording, but some fields have no other purpose than identification and others are useful as points of access. In the list given below,
the fields are labeled as searchable if the names given in the field
should be made into entries in a card catalog. An unsearchable field
indicates that no entry should be made except in a most unusual kind
of library.

Field One: Title (Searchable)

This field includes the uniform title, the conventional title, and any
secondary titles used to identify a work. Uniform title is very much
like a subject heading. It is a title established from a list and used
for very many different works whose identity can only be established
by key signature, thematic index numbers, and other means. In
serious music, a composition may be labeled only "Symphony" or
"Concerto for Piano and Orchestra" or "Sonata for Piano." Many
different composers have written symphonies, from Franz Josef Haydn
in the eighteenth century to Dmitri Shostakovitch in the twentieth. The
use of uniform titles resolves some of the problems of cataloging,
because there is always a title for a work regardless of the confusion
over what the composer called his work and how others have named it.

This field is the principal field of description and serves as the unit
entry. It is the irreducible minimum for all phonorecordings, and in
brief listing serves the library as the only entry, especially in combination with the second field. A later chapter includes a list of uniform
titles, and the precise way this can be used is described in the next
chapter. When cards are duplicated by multilith or mimeograph, the
uniform title is the first item on the card and field one is generally the
first line of the card. It is not a complete sentence, however, because
it may be necessary to include Fields two or three, depending on the
kind of phonorecording, as the concluding part of the minimum
description.

Field Two: Author, Composer (Searchable)

This field is for the composer of serious music, the author of plays,
the creator of a work in general. Matter to be included in Field two
should not be confused with that of Field three. The field is left
empty if the work is a collection and especially if the performer is the
most important person to be considered in the cataloging. Along with
Field three, the brief listing of phonorecordings is completed by
information in this field. Abbreviated cataloging may give the maximum
amount of information required by many different kinds of libraries,
including school collections, the collections in small or even medium-
size libraries. This field completes the initial sentence, or irreducible
minimum, of description.

Field Three: Performer (Searchable)

Along with title and composer, the performer is a possible element

for brief listing. With an appropriate abbreviation this field serves
as the second sentence of manually prepared, or computer-produced,
unit entry. These three fields are completely searchable, so that any
item included should appear as the entry line in a card catalog. As
indicated above, a combination of the first three fields will yield sufficient information for many library users. Other identifying information appears in Fields four and five.

Field Four: Producer
Field Five: Identifying Numbers (Unsearchable)

These are not searchable fields because the information contained
serves only to identify the phonorecording. By producer is meant the
individual responsible for the technical aspects of the item as well as
the recording company. The identifying numbers are matrix numbers
in subsequent pressings, used to establish the item. For locally
produced phonorecordings, the date may be supplied in place of the
identifying number, but this should not be confused with other significant dates, such as the date of a jazz performance. The information
in these fields may be omitted and the succeeding fields used instead
to identify the phonorecording.

Fields Six and Seven: Physical Description and Series
(Unsearchable)

In place of including information on the producer, the series note
can be used with the physical description to complete the identification
of a phonorecording where complete description is not necessary. This
is the limit of description in the Schwann Record and Tape Guide.
Physical description is limited to the barest essentials because there
is not great variety in types of phonorecordings: discs are simply
described by LP, for long-playing or microgroove, it being understood
that such phonodiscs are now standard and require a turntable that will
make 33 1/3 revolutions per minute. All other variations must be
more closely shown, such as 78 rpm, with the size of the disc. Tapes
can be identified as reels, tapes, cartridges, cassettes, etc. As
cartridges and cassettes are fully standardized, no further explanation
is needed. Reel-to-reel tapes will require a size designation, usually
in inches for the reel.

Series is often shown as the record company and the album number,
which is usually identical with the numbers on the phonorecordings.
The series designation may be used as a classification device, especially as the abbreviations and last three numbers of the series

description are quite sufficient to identify a particular phonorecording or album of discs. As can be seen, the series designation is often the same as the information included in Fields four and five, or so near as makes little difference. If any information is duplicated, then it is excessive for description and should be omitted. In a computerized system, the series field, Field seven, may be searchable so that Fields four and five should be left blank and information preferred in Field seven. However, Field seven is generally unsearchable and series information can be included in Fields four and five.

In brief listing, the information contained in Fields six and seven completes all the cataloging necessary to identify the phonorecording, providing no analysis is needed of the contents of the phonorecording. If analysis is needed, the following fields can be used, especially Field nine. A further consideration based on the need for analysis of the contents is the extent of description. Many libraries never describe the contents of phonorecording in detail beyond what is contained on one side of a phonodisc. Trying to pick up a particular band may result in damage to the phonorecording. It is much more practical to copy the contents of a single band (or cut) onto a cassette, a relatively easy task, than to try to play one band for a user in any kind of listening arrangement.

Fields Eight (Unsearchable) and Nine (Searchable)

These fields are reserved for analysis of the contents (Field nine) and for the additional items of description that may be necessary to further identify a phonorecording in a very large collection. Analysis of contents helps to identify a particular collection and may be necessary for a medium-size collection because users cannot always remember the title of the phonorecording containing exactly what they wish to hear. Additional description, Field eight, will be considered at length in the chapter devoted to this subject, but some general principles can be noted here.

A typical situation is to be observed in phonorecordings of operas. The librettist is usually unimportant to the average listener, although some were well-known authors in their own right. Furthermore, the story may derive from a famous play, as Verdi's Falstaff taken from the play The Merry Wives of Windsor by William Shakespeare. The libretto was written by Arrigo Boito (1842-1918). Although the librettist is not nearly so famous as the composer, Boito was in fact a musician of note and the composer of several works, especially the opera Mefistofele. Field eight would be used to bring out these facts, especially in a library of music in a college or university.

Field nine is devoted to an analysis of contents, and because phonodiscs are divided into sides and bands these words may be used in place of volumes and page numbers. With cassettes and cartridges the exact location of compositions is usually not so easily described. Reels are equally hard to designate, although extracts may be made onto small reels if necessary. The final method is to use a stop watch timed from the beginning of the phonorecording and play it through to locate each separate part as so many minutes and seconds from the beginning.

Field Ten: Added Entries and Subjects (Searchable)

In a computerized system there is no need to show the extent of entries to be made. The computer can search each field where entries are derived without any need to duplicate information already given. In a manual system much the same principle may be adopted if only those names that will serve as entries are included in the unit entry. Even so, not all the information useful as access to the phonorecording can be found in the entry. Although the need for subject headings is greatly reduced through the use of uniform titles, access to the collection by the instrument or the type of vocal music is often desirable. A categorized list of subject headings can be used by the technical assistant to provide full access to the collection of phonorecordings, so that even in a special music library full cataloging is possible with only occasional professional help.

If a great deal more is included in the description than is needed for entries, a selection must be made. This will require a listing of those parts of the catalog entry that will serve as access points for the user. As will be shown in the remainder of this chapter, the decision on what kind of catalog entry is necessary depends on the information that users wish to find in the catalog. Policy on the extent of cataloging must be established before the work actually begins. Even in a home collection. the owner should decide just what kind of records he wishes to keep of his phonorecording collection. They can be as simple or as elaborate as he finds most useful. The library is only a pooling of resources that might be found in individual homes, and it should provide access in the way the users would establish a separate catalog to get the most service from it.

EXAMPLES

Below are several kinds of phonorecordings with a transcription of information from the label and the information sorted into the various fields, followed by the same detail in card catalog format.

Cartridge: Label reads

Schubert
Moment Musical Op. 94 No. 5
Symphony No. 6 in C Maj.
The South German Philharmonic
Orchestra under the direction of
Alexander von Pitamic
Manufactured and distributed in the U.S.A.
and Canada under license from Polyband
Gesellschaft, Munich, Germany by
Casette Music Corporation, New York, N.Y.

On the narrow edge:

CMC   Schubert
8S525

On the other side:

8S525

Programs
Schubert: Moment Musical, Op. 94, no. 5 in F
1   Minor, Ernst Groschel, Piano.
Schubert: Symphony No. 6 in C Major (Little
C Major), Suddeutsche Philharmonic Orch.:
Alexander von Pitamic.
1. ADAGIO: ALLEGRO (Beg.)

2   1. ADAGIO: ALLEGRO (Concl.)
2. ANDANTE

3   3. SCHERZO: PRESTO
4. ALLEGRO MODERATO (Beg.)

4   4. ALLEGRO MODERATO (Concl.)

Fields:

1. Symphony 6, D. 589, C Major, "Little C Major"
2. by Franz Schubert, 1797 - 1828

3. Perf. by Alexander von Pitamic cond. Suddeutsche
   Philharmonic Orch.
4. Cassette Music, for Polyband Gesellschaft, Munich
5. CMC 8S525
6. Cartridge 8 Track Stereo
7. (Cassette Music Corporation CMC 8S525)
(8) (Omitted)
9. Track one: Moment Musical, Op. 94, no. 5; D. 780, 5; F
   Minor. Perf. by Ernst Groschel, Piano
   Track one: (Cont.) Adagio, Allegro, etc.
10. Piano & Orchestra. Orchestra.

Note that the major work has been cataloged here. The inclusion of
one of Schubert's Moments Musicaux is shown in the contents field.
Fields four and five are virtually repetitive of information in Field
seven.

In Field one, the number including the capital D. is the thematic
index number, called a Deutsch number after the musicologist who
provided this guide to the music of Schubert. This and Schubert's
dates have been added from Schwann Record and Tape Guide.

The entry given above is more elaborate than would be necessary for
a card catalog entry, but notice that all the information is included in
one place or another in the following example of the kind of unit card
that would be produced for this music:

> Symphony 6, D. 589, C Major, "Little C Major"
> by Franz Schubert. Perf. by Alexander von
> Pitamic cond. Suddeutsche Philharmonic Orch.
> Cassette Music Corp. for Polyband Gesellschaft,
> Munich.
> Cartridge 8 track stereo (CMC 8S525)
> Track one: Moment Musical, Op. 94, 5; D 780;
> F Minor. Perf. by Ernst Groschel, Piano.
> 1. Schubert, Franz, 1797-1828. 2. Pitamic,
> Alexander von. 3. Suddeutsche Philharmonic
> 4. Moment Musical, Op. 94, 5, D. 780, F Minor
> 5. Groschel, Ernst, Piano. 6. Piano & Orch.
> 7. Orchestra.

From this example and those to follow, several things can be seen.
The problem of multiple recordings in one container is commonplace
and rules must be established for determining when a unit entry will

serve and when several different entries are required. In this book, because it seems to be the most equitable practice involving least compromise and most accessibility, one side of a phonodisc will serve as the unit entry. A work that is contained within one side will be included as contents notes. The same is true for cassettes that must be turned over to be played through. Cartridges may be cataloged by the four tracks found on stereophonic recordings, but if a composition covers less than one of these tracks, it will be included as a contents note.

By comparing the entry for the computer with the card catalog unit entry, the problems of listing all the tracings can be seen. In some libraries, the tracings are always put on the verso of the card, with the first line nearest the hole, so that the entries can be read while the card is fixed in the catalog. The entry is quite long mostly because of duplication of information. Consider the following entry in a book catalog.

Symphony no. 6, "Little C Major," by Schubert.
    Alexander von Pitamic cond. Suddeutsche
    Philharmonic Orch.
    Cartridge 8 tr stereo (Cassette Music CSC 8S252)
    Tr 1: - Moment Musical, Op. 94, 5. Ernst Groschel,
    Piano.

All the important information is included and only the tracings are lacking. Just as a computer can be programmed to create lists by searching for various items in the entry, so a procedure for making additional entries can be designed to avoid the excessive repetition of names in the catalog entry, whether the information is put on cards or in a book catalog.

Brief listing would be even shorter as an entry, but in many libraries, especially school libraries, this is sufficient:

Schubert: Symphony no. 6, "Little C Major," and
    Moment Musical, Op. 94, 5. Cartridge CMC 8S252.

All mention of performers has been omitted, and because only one composer is represented in the phonotape, the work is entered under that composer. Brief listing by title with added listing for composer would analyze the phonorecording sufficiently for almost all home and school libraries. In this kind of collection care is taken to avoid duplication of the composition, because the primary interest of the user is in the music itself not in the performer. A music research library seeks to provide its users with a means of comparing performances so that many different interpretations of a work may be included. If the library contained nothing but phonorecordings of classical music each complete on one disc or on one tape, then entry by composer with added entries for performer and conventional titles would be sufficient and a very good means of organizing the collection.

The reason for specifying one composition per phonorecording can be understood by considering the following not at all unusual example. From a folded card that fits the plastic case, the following information can be derived:

9 CLASSICAL MASTERPIECES
7306 002
Philips

Rossini
La Gazza Ladra
Overture
Rimsky-Korsakov
Flight of the Bumble Bee
Raff
Cavatina
Strauss
Annen-Polka
and 5 other
classical masterpieces

Side 1:
GIUSEPPE VERDI (1813-1901)
CHORUS OF THE HEBREW SLAVES
"Va pensiero sull'ali dorate"
from "Nabucco"
Radio Chorus Leipzig
Dresden Philharmonic Orchestra
Herbert Kegel   *)

FELIX MENDELSSOHN Bartholdy
(1809-1847)
AUF FLUGELN DES GESANGES
op. 34, no. 2 (On Wings of Song)
(Heinrich Heine)
Radio Chorus, Leipzig
Herbert Kegel   *)
JOSEPH HELLMESBERGER (1855-1907)

BALL SCENES
Orchestra of the "Deutschlandsender"
Robert Hanell   *)

GIOACCHINO ROSSINI (1792-1868)
THE THIEVING MAGPIE
("La Gazza Ladra")
Overture
Lamoureux Orchestra
Robert Benzi
Side 2:
NICOLAY RIMSKY-KORSAKOV
(1844-1908)
FLIGHT OF THE BUMBLE BEE
from "The Tale of Czar Saltan" op. 57
Monte Carlo Opera Orchestra
Roberto Benzi
JOACHIM RAFF (1822-1882)
CAVATINA, op. 85 no. 3
Egon Morbitzer, violin
Radio Symphony Orchestra, Leipzig
Robert Hanell
GEORGES BIZET (1838-1875)
L'ARLESIENNE, SUITE No. 2
Farandole
(arr. Ernest Guiraud)
Lamoureux Orchestra
Igor Markevitch

DANIEL FRANCOIS ESPRIT AUBER
(1782-1871)
FRA DIAVOLO
Overture
Detroit Symphony Orchestra
Paul Paray
JOHANN STRAUS, jun. (1825-1899)
ANNEN-POLKA
Dresden Philharmonic Orchestra
Herbert Kegel   *)
*) Recorded by "VEB Deutsche Schallplatten, Berlin."

This card is readily lost and the label on the cassette gives only the
following information:

7306 002   Verdi: Chorus of the Hebrew Slaves (Piave) -
                Mendelssohn: Auf Flügeln des Gesanges -
PHILIPS   (Heine) - Hellmesberger: Ball Scenes -
                Rossini: La Gazza Ladra Overture

                                                                    1

7306 002   Rimsky-Korsakov: Flight of the Bumble Bee
                Raff: Cavatina - Bizet: Farandole (arr.
PHILIPS   Guiraud) - Auber: Fra Diavolo
                Overture - Strauss: Annen-Polka

                                                                    2

The label is firmly glued to the plastic of the cassette and would not
under ordinary circumstances be subject to destruction. A music research library would give thought to gluing the card onto the transparent
plastic container so that the information could be retained.

Phonorecordings of this kind can only be cataloged by using a uniform
title and the title on the work itself. Following the example established
above the computer input would be:

        Field   Description

        1.   Symphonic compositions "Nine Classical
                  Masterpieces."
        2.   omit
        3.   omit
        4.   Philips
        5.   7306 002
        6.   Cassette Stereo
        7.   (Philips 7306 002)
        8.   Jacket title
        9.   Side one: Verdi, "Chorus of the Hebrew Slaves," from
                  Nabucco, Kegel cond. Dresden Philharmonic, Radio
                  Chorus, Leipzig. - Mendelssohn, "Auf Fluegeln des
                  Gesanges," Op. 34, 2. - Hellmesberger, "Ball Scenes,"
                  Hanell cond. Orchestra of the Deutschlandsender. -
                  Rossini, Overture La Gazza Ladra Benzi cond.
                  Lamoureux Orch. -
                  Side two: Rimsky-Korsakov, "Flight of the bumblebee,"
                  Benzi cond. Monte Carlo Opera Orch. - Raff, "Cavatina."
                  Op. 85, 3, Morbitzer, Violin, Hanell cond. Radio
                  Symphony Orch. Leipzig. - Bizet, "Farandole" from
                  L'Arlesienne suite no. 2, Markevitch cond. Lamoureux
                  Orch. - Auber, Overture Fra Diavolo, Paray cond.

Detroit Symphony Orch. - Strauss, "Annen-Polka,"
Kegel cond. Dresden Philharmonic.
10.   Orchestra. Opera - Selections.

In the supplied information, Johann Strauss is misspelled. The
library must always determine its own rules of punctuation and capi-
talization, and it must correct the source if the information is incorrect.

If full cataloging were to be done for this cassette, there would be
some forty entries to include all the different titles and all the different
composers, performers, and the works from which the selections were
derived. Considering that these compositions are only a few minutes
in length, this would seem to be an extreme measure. If the selection
is the only example of the music, some libraries would have to do
complete analysis, but this is only a tedious not an intellectually chal-
lenging task. The ordinary library would find that the following entry
suffices:

Symphonic works - Collections, "Nine classical masterpieces."
Philips 7306 002.
Cassette Stereo
Compositions by Verdi, Mendelssohn, Hellmesberger, Rossini,
Rimsky-Korsakov, Raff, Bizet, Auber, and Strauss.

This example shows one kind of collection, where the principal
interest is in the type of music rather than in the performer or the
composer. All the works are very melodic and quite familiar. Such
collections abound in phonorecordings because many people enjoy
listening to music that does not demand attention and concentration.
The Muzak Corporation furnishes this kind of music, what one writer
called "chewing gum for the mind." The library of a television station
includes such phonorecordings in a section labelled "Mood Music," and
the library does well to make short work of the cataloging.

An example of a phonorecording of another kind has the following information on the label, omitting details of copyright and trade name
registration:

Decca Stereo
W. C. Fields
THE ORIGINAL VOICE TRACKS
FROM HIS GREATEST MOVIES
DL 79164   Side 1
7-11682
1. The philosophy of W. C. Fields

2. The "sound" of W. C. Fields
3. The rascality of W. C. Fields
4. The chicanery of W. C. Fields

Decca Stereo
W. C .Fields
THE ORIGINAL VOICE TRACKS
FROM HIS GREATEST MOVIES
DL 79164   Side 2
  7-11683
1. W. C. Fields - The braggart and teller of tall tales
2. The spirit of W. C. Fields
3. W. C. Fields - A man against children,
   motherhood, fatherhood, and brotherhood
4. W. C. Fields - Creator of weird names

This phonorecording exhibits one of the advantages deriving from Edison's invention. A performer dead for many years lives on in the sound of his voice, and the characteristic nasal twang of Fields impresses the public today with a comic genius as much as the public of yesterday enjoyed his approach to life, so much at variance with the canons of good behavior then and now. This is a collection based on a performer, who happens to be speaking rather than singing. Music is used to introduce the various parts, but it is of such little consequence that neither the orchestra's name nor its conductor deserves mention.

The computer input would be as follows:

Field	Description
1.	Comic monologues "W. C. Fields, the Original Voice Tracks from his Greatest Movies."
(2)	(omit)
3.	Fields, W. C. Comedian
4.	Decca Records
5.	7-11682, 3.
6.	12" LP Stereo
7.	(Decca 79164)
(8)	(omit)
(9)	(omit)
10.	Motion pictures - Selections

Fields actually wrote many of the lines included on this phonorecording, but it is not necessary to distinguish him as the author. Whoever wrote the narrative introduction and whoever performed it are as nameless as the musical group that fleshed out the selections from various movie sound tracks.

The catalog entry for a book catalog would be:

Comic monologues, "W. C. Fields, the original voice tracks from his greatest movies." Decca Records
12" LP Stereo (Decca 79164).
1. Fields, W. C. Comedian. 2. Motion picture - Selections.

In brief listing the uniform title is omitted as well as any further subject access, and utilizing a rule that permits the name to be rearranged so that the most important element comes first, the following is an entry for a library with a small collection:

Fields, W. C. The original voice tracks from his greatest movies. Decca 79164
12" LP Stereo

In both these examples, the listing of contents has been omitted, first because they are like the narrator and the musical group, only part of the presentation rather than useful in and of themselves, and second because it is highly unlikely that the user would come to the library with this information and no other. In any case, each of the sections of the phonodisc includes the name "W. C. Fields," so that the user with this information would find the phonorecording so long as an entry has been made under that name.

Another example worthy of consideration is the following:

VERVE   STEREO
Tape
Ella Fitzgerald Sings
THE RODGERS AND HART SONG BOOK

Arrangements and Orchestra Conducted by Buddy Bregman

Side 1

1. Have you met Miss Jones
2. You took advantage of me
3. A ship without a sail
4. This can't be love
5. The lady is a tramp
6. Manhattan
7. Johnny One Note
8. I wish I were in love again
9. Spring is here
10. It never entered my mind
11. Where or when
12. Little girl blue

Side 2

1. Give it back to the Indians	4. I didn't know what time it was	7. Bewitched
2. Ten cents a dance	5. I could write a book	8. My romance
3. There's a small hotel	6. My funny valentine	9. Wait till you see her
		10. Lover
		11. Isn't it romantic
		12. Blue moon

The information above is reproduced from the label glued onto the plastic reel containing quarter-inch tape for a reel-to-reel tape recorder. Such phonotapes are usually sold in a box that includes additional information, in this case the various musical comedies from which the songs were taken, with the exception of "Blue Moon." This song was the only one written and published simply as a popular song rather than as a part of a Broadway show. It was immensely popular when introduced in the 1930s and is still frequently sung. If the information is not needed, then the contents of the label are sufficient for the cataloging of the phonotape.

Field	Description
1.	Musical comedies - Selections "Ella Fitzgerald Sings the Rodgers and Hart Song Book."
2.	... Richard Rodgers, Composer, and Lorenz Hart, Lyricist.
3.	Perf. by Ella Fitzgerald, Vocalist; Buddy Bregman, Cond.
4.	Verve
5.	VST 4-205
6.	7" Reel Stereo
7.	(Verve VST 4-205)
8.	Arrangements by Buddy Bregman, Cond.
9.	Side one; Have you met Miss Jones; You took advantage of me; A ship without a sail; This can't be love; The lady is a tramp; Manhattan; Johnny One Note; I wish I were in love again; Spring is here; It never entered my mind; Where or when; Little girl blue. Side two: Give it back to the Indians; Ten cents a dance; There's a small hotel; I didn't know what time it was; I could write a book; My funny valentine; Bewitched; My romance; Wait till you see her; Lover; Isn't it romantic; Blue moon.
10.	Female Vocalists

In a computer entry, as noted elsewhere, it is not necessary to repeat the various names that are significant in this phonorecording. It is sufficient to list them in a way that is readily identified so that a relatively simple computer program can be written for the employment of such sophisticated equipment. Libraries that have not as yet begun to computerize their technical processes may employ just the signals given here, such as the three dots before the composer and the abbreviation "Perf. by" so that search strategies and listing routines can be simple and at the level of the unsophisticated user. A search strategy is a question put to the computer in such a way that the computer can locate the information desired. Libraries that have already begun to computerize their phonorecording catalog may have different methods of producing the input, that is, the information that is transcribed into machine-readable form for the computer to handle.

Such programs are capable of producing book catalogs and of providing special lists for patrons, so that the uniform title, serving much the same purpose as a subject heading, is especially useful. In manual procedures, the library may prefer to use the uniform title as a subject heading. The net effect is the same, except that a subject heading procedure based on the medium of the performer can work with the uniform title to give complete subject access to the work cataloged.

The entry for this work in a manual system, utilizing the rule for rearranging the name of the principal performer, would be as follows:

Fitzgerald, Ella "Sings the Rodgers and Hart Song Book." Music by Richard Rodgers, Lyrics by Lorenz Hart. Arr. and Cond. by Buddy Bregman. Verve VST 4-205
7" Reel Stereo.
1. Rodgers, Richard. 2. Hart, Lorenz. 3. Bregman, Buddy.

This catalog entry omits the listing of the various songs as well as a reference to the printed version of this work. It was published by Simon and Schuster in 1951. A library that files cards for phonorecordings in the same catalog with cards for books might want to include an entry to show that the printed Rodgers and Hart Song Book is also available in a performance by one of the most acclaimed of popular singers.

A further example of the kinds of phonorecordings and the way they are cataloged is considerably more complex. The label of this phonodisc is reproduced with a variation only in the type style used.

NATURAL HISTORY

MAGAZINE

The language and music of the wolves

Side 1   003   33 1/3 RPM Stereo

The Wolf You Never Knew

Narrated by Robert Redford

Script by Ron Holland

Produced by Bob Maxwell

Tonsil Records, New York, N. Y.

Lois Holland Callaway Entertainment Corp.

The flip side is exactly like the label for side one except that it is labelled "Side 2" and has the title "Sounds of the Wolf" omitting the narration of a script.

Side 2   ... Sounds of the Wolf

Produced by Bob Maxwell

Aside from the interesting contents of this phonorecording, reflecting the effort on the part of ecologists to create greater understanding of an unusual and at present endangered species, there are several problems of cataloging that would be almost insoluble if the rules for cataloging as given in the Anglo-American Cataloging Rules of 1967 were followed assiduously. What would the main entry be? Natural History Magazine? Robert Redford? Ron Holland? or possibly Bob Maxwell? At least on one side of the phonodisc, the performers are wolves living in the forests of Ontario, Michigan, and Minnesota.

In the examples given above, there has always been duplication in the fields for producer and identifying number with that included in the field for series. This phonorecording is an example where Fields four and five are most useful in sorting out information. Further, the use of uniform title, or subject heading, is rather clearer in this example than in others. A good procedure to adopt when a phonorecording is particularly puzzling is to begin with information that is easily ascertained, usually the physical description:

Field six: 12" LP Stereo

There is no series, unless Tonsil Records 003 is considered series. If so, then the producer and parent company can be placed in the appropriate fields for this information. The producer, however, has a position much like author, in which case we must account for the writer of the script narrated by Robert Redford. The division into fields solves most of the problems, and in particular it solves the crucial problem of what to place first. In a library of zoology the uniform title might be "Wolf howls" but in a collection of phonorecordings in a college library, the uniform title "Animal sounds" is specific enough for all practical purposes.

Field   Description

1.   Animal sounds. "The Language and Music of the Wolves."
2.   Produced by Bob Maxwell, Script by Ron Holland.
3.   Narrated by Robert Redford.
4.   Natural History Magazine in cooperation with Lois Holland Callaway Entertainment Corp.
5.   NHM - 003 A-6
6.   12" LP Stereo
7.   (Tonsil Records 003)
8.   American Museum of Natural History publishers of Natural History Magazine
9.   Side one: The wolf you never knew; Side two: Sounds of the wolf.
10. Natural History Magazine. American Museum of Natural History. Wolves.

Because Natural History Magazine and American Museum of Natural History are in unsearchable fields, the information must be a duplication in Field ten if the names are to be made part of a search strategy. A convenience of unsearchable fields is that information not required by the user does not need duplication in Field ten.

The next example shows the entry as it might appear in a book catalog (or differently spaced in a card catalog) for a library that would need all the information provided in the model computer input.

Animal sounds. "The language and music of the wolves." Produced by Bob Maxwell, script by Ron Holland, narrated by Robert Redford. Natural History Magazine in co-operation with Lois Holland Callaway Entertainment Corp. NHM-003 A-6 12" LP Stereo (Tonsil Records 003) American Museum of Natural History member's bonus Side one: "The wolf you never knew" Side two: "Sounds of the Wolf."
1. Maxwell, Bob 2. Holland, Ron 3. Redford, Robert, Narrator. 4. American Museum of Natural History.
5. Natural History Magazine. I. Wolves

It can be seen from this entry that the tracing reproduces information
contained in the entry in such a way that a rule for entering some information from the searchable fields would eliminate much of the
duplication. This entry is much more elaborate than would be required
in the ordinary school library. It is sufficient to identify the phonodisc
and provide some access to its contents:

> Animal sounds: "The language and music of the wolves" narrated
> by Robert Redford. Natural History Magazine
> 12" LP Stereo (Tonsil Records 003)
> Side 1, The wolf you never knew. Side 2, Sounds of the wolf.

A uniform title has been included in both these entries, although many
libraries would employ only the title of the phonorecording. If this is
the rule, then a rather elaborate and often confusing system of subject
heading is required.

SUMMARY

This chapter has explained the basic principles of description, the
means of identifying phonorecordings. These principles differ from
the descriptive cataluging of books in several ways. First of all, the
performer in the phonorecording is the key to establishing the extent
of the description required. As the examples showed, the performer
may be the whole purpose of the phonorecording (for instance, W. C.
Fields). The library must set a policy of what kind of cataloging is
going to be of most use to its patrons. The mechanics of producing
the catalog are important, but the method should not govern the extent
of the entry. If a computer is used, then the cataloging methods
should be such that elaborate programs requiring much computer time
are not necessary to gain access to information that can be assembled
using a simple program and little real time on the computer.

This first principle governs all the others. Once the extent of the
entry is known, then the cataloger can work very efficiently selecting
information from the label that will enable users of the library to find
precisely the phonorecording that meets their needs. No cataloger
must ever forget that his effort has the sole purpose of meeting the needs
of users. From this principle we derive the rule that the extent of
description is determined by the professional librarian after a careful
survey of his community and their needs.

In order to provide the essential elements of the briefly cataloged phonorecording, the cataloger must be able to identify all the elements and to rank these by their importance in providing subject access and identification.

This is accomplished by a wide knowledge of each of the fields of description, so that the cataloger would be able to provide complete input in a computerized system for a research library with an enormous collection of phonorecordings. Similarly, the cataloger should be able to recognize the relative importance of the fields and their contents so that the mimeographed list of phonorecordings typical of many school libraries will contain information that is readily understood and utilized by those to whom the list is distributed.

One word of warning is necessary. The library is cataloging for the future, not for the past. It is essential to predict how the library will grow and whether it will change. The methods suggested here have been extensively tried in computerized, mechanized, and manual systems. While it might seem that the necessity for uniform title is too little established as a device of cataloging, the theoretical principles underlying this procedure have been subjected to very rigorous testing. In deciding on a method of cataloging, the professional librarian must predict exactly what the use of the catalog will be. A good example was furnished the author recently in discussing how the phonorecording collection of an educational FM radio station should be organized. Access to the phonorecordings for the purpose of preparing programs to be broadcast required special attention to the composer of a work, the performers, and the time of each selection. A library technical assistant who has mastered the contents of this book would have no difficulty at all in creating the kind of catalog that the FM station will need, even though the rules for the preparation of cards for the catalog are apparently different from those found in this chapter. Actually, it is a primary decision of the professional librarian to establish the precise rules not only for the spacing and appearance of cards for a card catalog but also for showing what information will be included and in what order it shall be placed on the cards.

This is not a book of rules for cataloging phonorecordings. It is rather a means of understanding what such cataloging entails. A library that is in the process of organizing a collection of phonorecordings should investigate all the possibilities for providing maximum access that the users require with minimum effort. This second principle is derived from the first with the variations in library needs in mind.

First in the entry should be the field that will eliminate confusion and provide least duplication. It is not necessarily the same for all the different kinds of phonorecordings. Serious music can very well be entered under the composer with the unit entry always beginning with a composer's name. This is obviously unnecessary if the computer will be used to provide lists of phonorecordings arranged by whatever field is desired. A card catalog, however, is another proposition altogether. If only serious music is included, then arranging the unit entry so that the composer field, Field Two, is the entry line will eliminate duplication in the tracing and at least one card. As the number and kind of phonorecordings increase, especially if several different performances of a single work are available, this becomes an unreliable method of saving cards and space, because whatever is gained by the style of entry may be lost as the user requires help in order to search the card catalog for the information he needs.

The succeeding chapters of the first part of this book will proceed through the various fields, elaborating the definition and description included in this chapter with further examples and much explanation. When the reader has completed all these chapters, he should be able to catalog any phonorecording without hesitation or indecision. Just what field he makes the entry line and what fields he includes will be determined by the rules of the library in which he is employed. These are the only good rules for a cataloger to follow.

Chapter 8 then explains what may be found on Library of Congress cards, how this differs from other cataloging, and what kind of libraries can safely and efficiently use this cataloging. Chapter 9 gives the principles of development and examples of brief form entries.

Chapter 3

THE PROBLEM OF TITLE

The first field of description is reserved for the title of the phono-recording as found on the label fixed onto the item itself. This label cannot be readily removed and serves as the preferred location of all the descriptive material. However, in many cases, if not the majority, additional information must be taken from the protective covering of the phonorecording and from reference sources. The Schwann Catalog is so useful that it remains the preferred reference source.

Phonodiscs are usually packed in a paper sleeve and this is inserted into a jacket made of heavier paper, cardboard, or plastic-coated material. Sometimes all these materials are enclosed in a kind of box. The sleeve rarely includes usable information. The available space is often used for advertising material. The jacket, the outer covering of the fragile disc, is printed in vivid colors with drawings, photographs, and often a very carefully written explanation of the work.

The jacket serves as a most useful source of information, but it is not very durable. It can be lost, destroyed, or will simply wear out in time. However, if there is no title on the phonorecording itself, the title on the jacket can be used. A note must be made in Field Eight to show that the jacket is the source of the title used in the first field. Label title is not identified as such, because it is always the title employed where possible. The first problem that may be encountered is that the label does not furnish a title. Usually there is a title on the jacket, but in the event there is no title there either, a situation that may occur if the phonorecording is made by the library of another noncommercial source, a supplied title is used.

Supplied title means that the cataloger, usually a professional, or other authority will give the work a name. Many universities and historical societies make phonorecordings, usually in cassette form,

of interviews with local personalities in order to compile a history of
the region. Oral history, as it is called, is locally produced and
arrangements must be made so that each cassette is clearly labeled.
A title that is supplied for all such phonorecordings is a uniform title.
For oral history, the uniform title is often just the word "Interview,"
which not only identifies the type of recording but also serves to make
grammatical sense of the information that follows about the person
interviewed and the person who made the phonorecording and asked
the questions in the interview.

Uniform titles serve another important purpose. Often there are
several titles on a work, and much serious music has a title indicative
only of the form of the composition, so that it already has a kind of uniform title. Other works, however, have acquired additional titles,
sometimes employed by the composer, sometimes acquired from critics
or the public. These titles represent a kind of agreement among
music lovers and are called conventional titles. It is not unusual to
find phonorecordings that include a label title with a conventional title
and a jacket title that differs entirely. An abundance of titles is just
as much a problem as a lack of any. To resolve this problem, uniform
titles are used for all the phonorecordings, so that whatever the problem,
there will always be a title for the phonorecording. Title serves as the
principal means of identifying a phonorecording, and it also complements
the subject heading in providing a uniform approach to compositions as
well as phonorecordings. The two are not the same. A phonorecording
may include several compositions, parts of a composition, or a special
version of a composition, so that the title of the work as it appears on
the score played by the musician is not always the same as the title
used by the producer of the phonorecording.

A uniform title is taken from a list employed by the cataloger in order
to provide a uniform approach to the contents of the phonorecording.
A list of uniform titles is provided in Chapter Seven. The use of uniform titles resolves a very difficult problem of subject analysis.
Subject headings used by the Library of Congress include both form of
composition and instruments that perform it in one subject heading.
This makes it very difficult for the user of the subject portion of the
catalog to locate the information he wants, and it makes the list of
subject headings for music very long and confusing. In the Library of
Congress, the music section uses a classified catalog which minimizes
the problems that arise from the subject headings.

In brief-form cataloging, the uniform titles can be used as subject
headings along with the list of subject headings also provided in
Chapter Seven. The uniform titles can be used to categorize a

collection of phonorecordings, with each serving as a heading in a book catalog and the different compositions listed under the heading.

In complete cataloging, the uniform title is the first element in Field One. This will be most useful in programming a computer for direct (on-line) searches. The lack of uniformity in titles is eradicated, so that a simple coding system can be devised to locate all the phono-recordings in a large collection. If the computer is used to produce cards, the result in the card file will be a unit card that includes all the information a user needs in the sequence that will make examining the card more rapid and effective.

The result in a manual system is exactly the same if a card file of phonorecordings is maintained. When the collection is growing or changing, the card-file method is most effective. Cards may be added anywhere, providing what is called random access for additions, so that the card file can be as up-to-date as the cataloging itself. Unit cards can be produced by mimeograph or multilith and the many entries needed added as necessary. A computer can be programmed to add entries as desired. In any case, the result can best be shown by examples.

Example 1

Jacket:
       An International Triumph   Andre Watts/Leonard Bernstein
          Brahms Piano Concerto No. 2 in B Flat/New York Philharmonic
Label:
       Brahms: Concerto in B-flat Major for Piano and Orchestra, no. 2,
          Op. 83.

The words "An International Triumph" cannot be considered the title of the phonorecording. The label does not mention this, and it is safe to assume that these words amount to advertising copy meant to sell the phonorecording.

Example 2

Label title:
         Sibelius
       SYMPHONY No. 2 IN D, op. 43.

This phonodisc includes several elements necessary to identify the composition (and the phonorecording):

Symphony is a uniform title. It indicates the form of the composition.
No. 2 is the number of this work in the list of symphonies composed by Sibelius.

IN D gives the musical key. Musicians use this to identify the
Symphony.
   It is more reliable than the number, which may be incorrect or
   misleading.
Op. 43 is the opus number. Opus is a Latin word meaning "work."
   The opus number is established by musicologists, if not the composer himself, and indicates the number of the work when placed
   among all the composer wrote. These numbers are usually
   assigned in chronological order.

Rule for Serious Music:

   The title is arranged so that the uniform title comes first, then the
musical key, then the number of the form, then the opus number.

For this phonodisc, Field One would be prepared in this fashion:
   Field One: Symphony, in D, no. 2, Op. 43.

   Added entries would be made for the composer, Jean Sibelius, for
the conductor, Leopold Stokowski, and for the orchestra, the NBC
Symphony Orchestra, so that the first two lines of these entries would
appear as follows:

Sibelius, Jean, 1865-1957.   Sibelius, Jean Christian,
   Symphony in D, no. 2, Op. 43   1865-1957.
                                                            Symphony in D, No. 2,
Stokowski, Leopold, Cond.   Op. 43....
   Symphony in D, no. 2, Op. 43....

NBC Symphony Orchestra
   Symphony in D, no. 2, Op. 43....

   The subject heading for this work would be Orchestra. This entry
would complete all required access points even in the most thorough
system:

Orchestra
   Symphony in D, no. 2, Op. 43....

Example 3

Label title:
      Wolfgang Amadeus MOZART
      SYMPHONY No. 41 in C Major, K. 551.
         "Jupiter"

   The word "Jupiter" is a conventional title, given to this symphony by
some unknown listener. The jacket describes the conventional title as
a "nickname." In any case, Mozart's Jupiter Symphony would be

familiar to anyone who likes serious music. In the strict sense, it is "classical" music. The number K. 551 is an opus number of a special type. It is a Koechel number, named for the musicologist who provided opus numbers for Mozart's works. This is a very difficult task, but it is necessary when the composer has left incomplete records or has badly misnumbered his own works. It serves as the opus number for Mozart's work only. A few other composers, Bach and Schubert, for example, have special opus number systems. The K. number is used just like an opus number for purposes of identifying the work.

The conventional title is always given immediately after the opus so that the entry would read:

Symphony in C   No. 41, K. 551, "Jupiter..."

We must augment our rule for serious music to include a conventional title.

Rule for Serious Music:

The title field is arranged so that the uniform title comes first, then the musical key, then the number of the form, then the opus number. Conventional title, if any, follows the uniform title, the musical key, number of the work in the same form, and opus number.

An added entry would be made for the conventional title, so that in addition to entries for Mozart, Wolfgang Amadeus, 1756-1791, there would be an entry as follows:

"Jupiter"
Symphony in C   No. 41, K. 551, "Jupiter..."

Notice that in a unit-entry system, the word is repeated. Because the cards are reproduced all at a time, it would be an unnecessary amount of effort to remove the word. If each entry were separately typed, there would be no need to repeat the word "Jupiter."

On the flip side of this phonodisc there is another composition by another composer. Because the works are shown independently as each side of a phonodisc is cataloged, the work would have a separate entry.

Example 4

Label title:
    Franz Joseph HAYDN
    SYMPHONY No. 94 in G Major
        "Surprise"

Notice that the opus number has been omitted. The number of the symphony is sufficient. This work, too, has a conventional title acquired because of the sudden fortissimo passage in the second movement. At the first performance on March 23, 1792, the surprise so delighted the audience that the second movement was played again as an encore. The title field would be given as follows:

Field One: Symphony in G   no. 94, "Surprise"...

Some libraries would make an effort to find the opus number or its equivalent for this work. If the number of the form identifies the work sufficiently, the opus number may be of secondary importance. It can be omitted safely here, though that is not always the case.

Example 5

This example requires that the label be copied in some detail even though much of it would not be put into Field One.

CONCERTO IN D MAJOR
(Beethoven, Op. 61)

First Movement: Allegro ma non troppo

DAVID OISTRAKH (Violin) and the
STOCKHOLM FESTIVAL ORCHESTRA
     Conducted by
SIXTEN EHRLING

A concerto is a composition for a solo instrument with orchestral accompaniment, usually a full symphony orchestra. It is necessary to show in the title field what the solo instrument is. If the accompaniment is a symphony orchestra, the word "orchestra" does not need to be included. For this example, Field One would be as follows:

Field One: Concerto for Violin in D   Op. 61, ... etc.

Example 6

On the jacket of this phonorecording is the following information:

MILSTEIN
Prokofiev: The Two Concertos for Violin & Orchestra...

On the label, however, this information is not repeated:

Side 1   36009
   PROKOFIEV
CONCERTO NO. 1 IN D MAJOR, Op. 19
....
     NATHAN MILSTEIN, Violinist

Information about the tempi of the various movements has been omitted. In cataloging this phonorecording, it is not necessary to include the jacket title because that simply duplicates what is given on each side of the phonorecording.

Field One: Concerto for violin in D Major, Op. 19....

This would be the cataloging for Side 1 of the phonodisc. A note would be made in Field Nine to show that the other side was another work.

Example 7

    On the jacket is the title   TEN TENORS
                                    TEN ARIAS

However, there is no such title on the label of the phonorecording. In this case, the jacket title so neatly summarizes the phonorecording that it is included. The uniform title is "Operatic areas," so that Field One would be as follows:

Field One: Operatic arias   "Ten Tenors. Ten Arias"...

    Lacking the jacket title, it would be necessary to catalog the first aria to serve as identification for the whole phonorecording. This is a measure to be employed as a last resort and avoided where possible because it leads to a certain amount of confusion, and it is not suited to brief-form cataloging.

    Operas, some symphonic works, operettas, musical comedies, and ballet scores have definite titles, given by the composer to the work he writes, or at least the librettist. Such works might seem to be exceptions to the rule that would include a uniform title for serious music. However, at least for the unit card, the uniform title serves to identify the work completely. For example, operas are recorded in their entirety and phonorecordings of the whole work are available, but in most cases extracts of the more impressive passages will be included in a single phonorecording. The uniform title would be Opera for the entire work and Opera-Selections for the extracts, or highlights as such collections are often labeled.

Example 8

        Wagner
    TRISTAN AND ISOLDE

    Field One: Opera   Tristan and Isolde ...

Works with a definite title do not require opus numbers or key indication for identification. It is sufficient to give both the uniform title

and the title of the work.   The title most commonly used is employed.
Thus Tristan and Isolde is preferable in libraries where the clientele
speak English to Tristan und Isolde, the actual title given the work by
Richard Wagner.   However, it would be wrong to give the title The
Troubadour to the opera Il Trovatore by Guiseppe Verdi and even worse
to entitle La Traviata, The One who Found Herself.

Highlights from Tristan and Isolde would be shown as:

    Field One: Opera-Selections from   Tristan and Isolde ...

Example 9

When a question exists whether a work is a symphony with a title or is
something like a symphony, the uniform title "Symphonic work" can be
employed.   This is different from the term "-Selections", but it serves
much the same purpose.   For example,

    Field One: Symphonic work   "Harold in Italy" ...

would be used for a phonorecording entitled "Harold in Italy."   This
work is not quite a concerto for viola and orchestra and not quite a
symphony.   The opus number would not be included because the work
has a definite title.   If desired, it should precede the title of the work.

Example 10

    Similarly, the following is not quite a song cycle and not exactly a
symphony:

    Field One: Symphonic Work   "Das Lied von der Erde," (1908)...

This work does not have a readily available opus number.   The date of
completion of the work may be given in lieu of an opus number for
Mahler's works, following the title of the work.

Example 11

    Some extracts from longer works become better known than the original
work, such as overtures to operas and ballets.   For instance,

Label title:
        Berlioz
    FOUR OVERTURES
Jacket title:
        Hector Berlioz
    Four Overtures

    Field One: Overtures   "Four Overtures" ...

is the entry for the phonorecording.   Some libraries would want to include the two overtures on one side in field one.

    Field One: Overtures   Four Overtures: "The Corsair," Op. 21; "The Roman Carnival," Op. 9 ...

Example 12

Musical comedies and motion picture sound tracks are frequently recorded, featuring all the important songs.

    Field One: Musical comedy   Out of this World ...

American libraries might reduce the uniform title to Musical.

The same score may be both a musical comedy and a motion picture. The rules of the library would determine whether the phonorecordings should receive the same or different uniform titles. In a unit-entry system where many entries are made, the conventional title will bring together the various recordings.

Example 13

    Field One: Musical comedy   Oklahoma ...

or

    Field One: (Motion Picture) Sound Track   Oklahoma ...

Example 14

Suites prepared from ballets differ from the score used in the performance. There is much greater repetition in the actual music played for dancers than in the music prepared for performance as an independently enjoyable composition. It is not necessary to indicate that the phonorecording is made up of selections. The uniform title Ballet is sufficient indication that not every part of the ballet music is included. Sometimes there are several different versions, as in the phonorecordings made of Tchaikovsky's ballet The Nutcracker, for which there exist two suites as well as the complete ballet music.

    Field One: Ballet   The Nutcracker ...

    Field One: Ballet   The Nutcracker, Suite no. 1 ...

    Field One: Ballet   The Nutcracker, Suite no. 2 ...

This shows the first field of three different phonorecordings.

Popular music on 12" long-playing phonodiscs may have no title at all, substituting the performer's name for the title.

Example 15

Label title:
> PAT BOONE
> with Orchestra

Jacket title:
> PAT BOONE

The uniform title for such a work preserves the field for cataloging purposes. Fields Two and Three can be omitted and the contents of Field One limited to the uniform title and the title of the phonorecording.

> Field One: Popular songs   "Pat Boone" . . .

Example 16

Similarly

> Field One: Popular songs   "Tiny Tim's 2nd Album" . . .

With subsequent albums, new titles will be found. A collection of popular music usually features a performer. The first album may use the performer's name as a title and the second make the performer the center of attraction in some other way.

Example 17

Label title:
> Pat's Great Hits

> Field One: Popular Songs   "Pat's great hits"

This is another phonorecording of a collection of songs sung by Pat Boone.

Example 18

> Field One: Popular music   "Whipped cream and other delights,"
> a collection of compositions played by Herb Alpert and his
> Tijuana Brass.

Jazz is very much like popular music in that the performer is the most important feature of the phonorecording. Libraries that specialize in music of this kind would develop an elaborate list of uniform titles, or subject headings, to indicate precisely what kind of music is available. Similarly, libraries of recorded speech will develop special uniform titles to create categories of phonorecordings that fit into their speciality.

Example 19

Label title:

> Carolina
> Low country Patois
> GULLAH
> in story and rhyme by

Field One: English dialects   "Gullah: Carolina lowcountry
patois"

This exemplifies a necessary corollary to the rule for Field One.
The cataloger must rearrange elements in the title so that the most
important elements come first. In the examples of serious music,
regardless of how key indication and opus number appeared on the
phonodisc label, the pattern of uniform title, key indication, opus
number or equivalent, and conventional title was standard throughout.

Example 20

Label title:

> KERMIT SCHAFER PRODUCTIONS
> Presents
> (THE BLOOPY AWARDS)
> (For Broadcasting's Classic Bloopers)

Field One: Humor   "The Bloopy Awards for broadcasting's
classic bloopers"

The punctuation of the entry follows rules established by the library
rather than the punctuation, if any, found on the phonorecording label.

Example 21

Phonorecordings of almost everything can be found or made, from
sound effects to Mahler's Symphony of a Thousand, which is well named
because a vast assemblage of choruses and orchestra with soloists is
required to perform it. Sound effects, unless they are the principal
type of phonorecording collected, can be cataloged like any other.

Label title:

> NATURAL HISTORY
> MAGAZINE
> The language and music of the wolves

Field One: Animal sounds   "The language and music of the
wolves" ...

Example 22

Many of these examples are collections of works, for instance the
popular songs, although such works are also issued in single recordings,
often in 7 inch size with 45 RPM speed.

Label title:
>   OUR LAST GOODBYE
>   from the Columbia Lp "HONEY" CS 9662

>   Field One: Popular song   "Our last goodbye" ...

In Field Eight a note would be made that would refer the user to the
Columbia long-playing phonodisc from which this selection was taken.
In Field Nine the contents of the flip side would be given:

>   Field Nine: With "Happy heart" ...

Similarly the following example:

Example 23

Label title: (Poor Old) MR. JENSEN

>   Field One: Popular song   "Poor Old Mr. Jensen," ...

>   Field Nine: With "May I take a giant step into your heart" ...

Further examples will be found in Chapter 7 which discusses Notes and
Content Analysis.

SUMMARY

Unit entry rule for Field One: In this field the following elements
are included in this order if all are present:

1. Uniform title, supplied by a list kept by the librarian. The
    uniform title may be the only title a work has.
2. Uniform title may be amplified by key indication, number of kind
    of work, opus number, and number of the work if it is part of a
    longer opus.
3. Conventional title always follows the uniform title and all that
    pertains to it (key indication and opus number).
4. If there is no key indication, only a uniform title supplied from
    the list and not found in the title of the work, the opus number
    follows the conventional title.
5. A label title is used after the uniform title for "collections of
    works."
6. A jacket title is used after the uniform title if there is no label
    title. This is noted in Field Eight, "Additional description."
7. Entries are made for the conventional title and for the label title
    or jacket title. No entry is made for the key indication or opus
    number.

BRIEF-FORM CATALOGING

A single-entry system requires that the elements be arranged in the order of their importance. As explained in the preceding chapter, the contents of Fields One, Two, Three, and Four in reduced form suffice. The unifying element must be placed first. If there is the performer, as in Example 15 (Pat Boone) this would be put first. But an order of precedence is important where composer, performer, and title of composition are all given. For instance, the phonorecording cited in Example 9:

Label title:

Berlioz   Side 1
HAROLD IN ITALY, Op. 16
Band 1 - First Movement: Harold in the Mountains
Band 2 - March of the Pilgrims
William Primrose, Violist
Boston Symphony Orchestra
Charles Munch
Conductor.

For serious music the order is always

Composer, Title of composition, Soloist performer, Conductor, and Orchestra.

The entry would be:

Berlioz: "Harold in Italy" Primrose, Charles Munch cond.
Boston Symphony Orchestra ...

The uniform title would be used to categorize the different compositions so that this entry would be found in the section entitled "Symphonic Works." No added entries are made, although it is possible to number the entries so that each has a unique identifying number and then to provide an index to each entry as full as desired, listing performers, composers, and conventional titles in separate indexes.

Succeeding chapters will establish the contents of the remaining fields for the works noted as examples and others that will illustrate the nature of phonorecordings.

Chapter 4

COMPOSERS, AUTHORS, COMPILERS

The Schwann Record and Tape Guide lists phonorecordings by composer.
In general this suits most collectors of serious music, who are likely
to know a great deal about the composers of music through the ages.
All the major composers are subjects of biographies, sometimes several, and there are scores of reference works on music listing the
composers and giving both detail of their lives and explanations of their
works.

In the unit-entry system explained here, the composer appears as
entry for all works that clearly indicate who the composer is. With
serious music this is not much of a problem, except for operas. The
words sung in an opera are written by a poet, because verse is much
easier to sing than prose. These words make a little book, the Italian
word for which has become standard for referring to the words of an
opera: the libretto. The author is called the librettist. Some have
been very famous, such as Arrigo Boito, a composer in his own right,
who wrote the libretti (the plural of libretto) for Verdi's last two operas,
Otello and Falstaff. Richard Wagner wrote his own libretti, because
he considered himself to be at least as great a poet as he was a musician. Lorenzo da Ponte, who wrote the libretto for Don Giovanni by
Mozart, was very well known. Even though the names seem strange
to English-speaking people, many were important poets and dramatists
whose writings were in French, German, or Italian. Eugene Scribe,
Emile Zola, Hugo von Hofmannsthal, Bertolt Brecht, Felice Romani,
and Francesco Maria Piave became famous as much for their libretti
as for their other works. Scribe was a dramatist of note and Zola a
very important novelist. The few successful American operas have
been written by Gertrude Stein, famous for her obscurantist later
writings, W. H. Auden, and John LaTouche.

For the most part, librettists are harmless drudges, deserving

49

Samuel Johnson's definition of lexicographers. Even though the book
Tenth Muse, by Patrick J. Smith (New York: Knopf, 1970) is devoted
to the writing of libretti, only the most studious of opera fans remember
who wrote the words and why.

Sometimes words written for a different purpose are used by a
composer. Beethoven used the words to a famous poem by Schiller in
the choral movement, the fourth, of his last symphony. A German
translation of the Chinese poetry of Li Tai Po was set to music by
Gustav Mahler in his work Das Lied von der Erde. Arrigo Boito obtained the story for Otello from the play Othello, by Shakespeare, and
Falstaff is a musical version of Shakespeare's Merry Wives of Windsor.
Spanish and French dramas have furnished many libretti; for instance,
Angel de Saavedra, Duke of Rivas, wrote La Fuerza del Sino which
became La Forza del Destino with music by Verdi.

Sometimes a composition is rearranged by another musician. Johann
Sebastian Bach wrote great music for the organ, much loved by organists
and those who enjoyed listening to serious organ music. Leopold
Stokowski, a conductor, transcribed some of this music for full symphony orchestra. Toccata in D Minor was one of his transcriptions and
was included in the Walt Disney film Fantasia. Beethoven prepared his
own piano version of his violin concerto.

Almost every conductor provides his own interpretation of a work,
and some operas are customarily cut in time-honored ways in performance. In a scene of The Barber of Seville, the soprano, Rosina, is
being given a music lesson. For years it was customary for the soprano
to substitute another aria for the one that Rossini wrote. In the old-
style concerto, the performer was supposed to improvise his own solo
passage, usually performed in the first movement. This cadenza was
meant to display the soloist's virtuosity, and a few such cadenzas have
become very famous, for instance, the Joachim cadenza for Beethoven's
violin concerto.

Complexity of entry does not serve a purpose if it does not further the
identification of the music. Arrangers who work with popular singers
are responsible for the orchestration. They may be given credit on
the label of a phonodisc, but since a singer is more important than the
arranger of the music, the identification of the performer may not
indicate the arrangement as well. Some judgement has to govern
whether an arranger is included in Field Two. Even a librettist may
be omitted in some library cataloging of recorded operas. The rela-
tionship of the opera to another literary work will depend on the
procedures established in a given library. Field Eight is reserved

for additional information for which no additional entry will be made.
A college library might wish to note that Wether by Jules Massenet is
taken from Goethe's Leiden des Jungen Werther. Nothing important
would be lost if this piece of information were left to music majors to
discover as a part of their research. A catalog card is not a substitute
for reference books.

A good rule is that where a possibility of confusion exists, full information about the creators of a work is desirable in complete
cataloging. Hence, the librettist ought to be included routinely.
Princess Ida is an opera by Gilbert and Sullivan. To include only Sir
Arthur Sullivan would be misleading. He wrote a lengthy and serious
work, entitled Ivanhoe, that is not performed now at all partly because
of its heavily sentimental libretto. Everyone thinks of the comic operas,
or operettas, as by Gilbert and Sullivan, even though few people think
of Aida by Ghislanzoni and Verdi. If the librettist must be included for
some works, then it is better to include the name for all operas rather
than try to work out a pattern of exceptions one way or the other. It
is better to leave the librettist out, in every case, or include the
librettist in every case.

Major revisions, such as transcribing an organ work for symphony
orchestra or transforming a violin concerto into a piano concerto
deserve to be noted as well. Where the arranger is of secondary importance and does not help to identify the composition, his name may
safely be omitted.

Composers and lyricists of popular music have come to be as well
known as other musicians. Richard Rodgers and Lorenz Hart wrote
many musical comedies together, so that a book of their songs has been
published, and there are dozens of recordings of the songs. Ella
Fitzgerald recorded The Rodgers and Hart Song Book, including almost
all the memorable music that Rodgers wrote to words by Lorenz Hart.
After Hart died, Rodgers wrote music for musical comedies for which
Oscar Hammerstein II furnished the lyrics. Rodgers and Hammerstein
became as well known as Gilbert and Sullivan. If only Richard Rodgers
were identified, there would be no way to distinguish between two quite
different kinds of musical comedies.

Popular groups often compose their own lyrics. The Beatles, for
instance, write their own songs, and some of these are not only fine
music but also beautiful poetry. Other groups sing the music of other
composers, so that an order of priority must be established in Fields
One, Two, and Three. Field One, the title, takes preference over all
other fields; then Field Two, Creator, Composer, Lyricist, then

Field Three, Performer. There is no need to repeat a name as composer-arranger and performer. If the whole phonorecording is named for the person who was all three, then entering the title of the phonorecording after the uniform title will adequately indicate to the user what the item cataloged is.

Spoken works, such as plays, readings of verse, addresses, orations, and interviews are very much like books in that there is an author who may also be the performer, a poet reading his own verse, or a famous man whose speeches were recorded as he spoke them, such as President John F. Kennedy giving his Inaugural Address, or President Franklin D. Roosevelt giving his first Inaugural Address or his "Fireside Chats." Natural language is usually more meaningful in spoken form, and historians like to hear the phrasing, emphasis, pauses, and intonation that add meaning to words in spoken form and that cannot be readily reproduced in written form. A research collection in a university library devoted to history may include all possible such phonorecordings.

The university may also include research into the region in phonorecordings through interviews with residents who have good memories and like to talk. They could not be persuaded to write down their reflections, because of the constraints of preparing English prose, but they will add greatly to the historian's fund of primary source material. This is oral history, as mentioned before, and the question of who is the author and who is the performer can be baffling. The priorities given above still prevail. After the uniform title "Interview" the name of the person being interviewed and then the interviewer fill Fields One and Two. Field Three can be omitted because all necessary information is contained in the first two fields.

Dramatic works require a cast and a director, so that all three fields will be utilized. A decision must be made whether all the actors will be included in Field Three or only a few, but the author must be included in Field Two. Authors are a principal means of identification of any written work.

A much more common problem is that several different compositions by one composer or by several composers are included on one phonorecording. Many of the examples cited earlier in this book are of this type. The problems of cataloging these phonorecordings must be resolved, in the beginning, by the policy of the library. There are several options. Using a uniform title, the cataloger can look for the unifying element, either type of composition, composer, or performer. Almost all phonorecordings can be cataloged in such a way that the featured element is emphasized. In considering this kind of phonorecording above, the use of uniform title as the unifying element was shown, and

this combined with the title permits the cataloging of even the most
heterogeneous of collections, with many different composers, compositions, and performers included in one item.

Another method of simplification discussed is the cataloging of
phonorecordings one side at a time, or one track at a time for cartridges.
Phonodiscs, phonocassettes, and phonotape in reel form, can be considered to have sides. If one side is cataloged, the variety of works
included is at least halved. So far as composer is concerned, this
can represent a further unifying element. In the next chapter, it will
be seen that the performer represents another opportunity to catalog
the phonorecording. The following examples demonstrate how the
unifying element and cataloging one side at a time resolve some of the
problems of phonodiscs.

Example 1

Label titles:
    SIDE 1
                        Beethoven
        CONCERTO IN C MAJOR, OP. 56

    First Movement: Allegro-Piu Allegro

    SIDE 2
                        Beethoven
        CONCERTO IN C MAJOR, OP. 56

    Second Movement: Largo

    Third Movement: Rondo al Polocca - Allegro - Tempo 1

Jacket Title:
    BEETHOVEN: Triple Concerto in C Major, Op. 56
    DAVID OISTRAKH TRIO....

This work should be considered one composition on two sides of a
phonodisc. The word "triple" in its title refers to the number of instruments not the number of movements or the three tempo notations
in the third movement. The cataloging is fairly straightforward:

    Fields One and Two:
    Concerto for violin, cello, and piano in C, Op. 56, "Triple..." by
        Ludwig van Beethoven.

Elsewhere in the catalog entry the performers would be cited, including
the members of the David Oistrakh Trio and the Conductor as well as
the symphony orchestra.

Example 2

Label title:

BEETHOVEN

QUARTET IN E FLAT, OPUS 74

SIDE 1

BEETHOVEN

QUARTET IN F MINOR, OPUS 95

SIDE 2

Unlike the previous example, this work contains two separate compositions. Cataloging each side, however, reduces the problem to the vanishing point. Field Six, used for physical description, would include the information that just one side was included in the description of the contents of this phonodisc. The real problem with this item is that it lacks necessary information to complete Field One, the title of the phonorecording. Fortunately the information about the works printed on the reverse of the jacket supplies some of what is missing, and the handy Schwann Record and Tape Guide supplies the rest:

Fields One and Two:

Quartet for strings in E Flat, no. 10, Op. 74, "Harp..." by
Ludwig van Beethoven.

Fields One and Two:
Quartet for strongs in F Minor, no. 11, Op. 95, "Serioso..." by
Ludwig van Beethoven.

A user searching for music by Beethoven would find all these compositions under the heading, Beethoven, Ludwig van, 1770-1827. The Schwann catalog furnishes the dates for composers, omitting this information only when it is unknown or very difficult to determine.

Composer entries:
Beethoven, Ludwig van, 1770-1827
Concerto for violin in C Major, "Triple..." Op. 56, by Ludwig
van Beethoven.

Beethoven, Ludwig van, 1770-1827
Quartet for strings in E Flat, no. 10, Op. 74, "Harp..." by
Ludwig van Beethoven.

Beethoven, Ludwig van, 1770-1827
Quartet for strings in F Minor, no. 11, Op. 95, "Serioso..." by
Ludwig van Beethoven.

The following example is characteristic of a large number of phonodiscs. The composition recorded is not long enough to fill up both

sides but too long for just one side of a phonorecording. Another
composition is included, but it is less than one side of a phonorecording.

Example 3

Label title:
SIDE 1
SIBELIUS
SYMPHONY NO. 5 IN E FLAT MAJOR, OP. 82

SIDE 2
SIBELIUS
SYMPHONY NO. 5 IN E FLAT MAJOR, OP. 82
1 - Third Movement: Allegro molto
2 - FINLANDIA, Symphonic poem, Op. 26

The problem is worse than it looks, and it is taken care of in fields
other than the First and Second. In Field Six, the physical description
would include information that the symphony is on side one and band one
of side two. The symphonic poem would be described as Side 2, Bd. 2.
It could be cataloged separately, however, and a note included in
Field Nine to indicate that it is included in a phonodisc otherwise devoted to Symphony no. 5. Many libraries try to avoid the possible
damage that comes from setting a needle down in the middle of the
phonodisc. Even though a blank space separates the bands, steady hands
and great care are required not to mar the phonodisc. Field Nine exists
to show the contents of a phonorecording and because entries are made
for all the significant elements included in this field, there is no need
for a separate entry for the symphonic poem.

Composer entry:
Sibelius, Jean, 1865-1957
Symphony in E Flat Major, no. 5, Op. 82, by Jean Sibelius.

Added title entry:
"Finlandia"
Symphonic poem, Op. 26, with Symphony in E Flat Major, no. 5,
Op. 82, by Jean Sibelius.

Note that the unit card begins with the word Symphony.

Fields One and Two:
Symphony in E flat Major, no. 5, Op. 82, by Jean Sibelius.

This method is especially useful when several different works are
included in the same phonodisc. Full access to the individual works
is gained without the necessity of providing different unit entries. The
same card may be used for all the different compositions. The

following example is also characteristic of many phonodiscs. There
is no other way to record short compositions on a twelve-inch long-
playing disc.

Example 4

Label title:
    Side 1
    WEBER
        1. Clarinet Concerto no. 1 in F Minor, Op. 73 ...
        2. Concertino for Clarinet and Orchestra, Op. 26 ...
    Side 2
    WEBER
        1. Quintet in B-flat Major for Clarinet and Strings, Op. 34

The simplest method of cataloging this phonorecording is to accept
the composer as the unifying element and to make a unit entry for
each of the two sides. The unit entry for Side 1 will be as follows:

Fields One and Two:
Concerto for clarinet in F Minor, no. 1, Op. 73, by Carl Maria
    von Weber.

Fields One and Two:
Quintet for clarinet and strings in B flat Major, Op. 34, by Carl
    Maria von Weber.

Field Nine would not be used because the Quintet occupies one full side.
Field Nine for the flipside would be as follows:

Field Nine:
Contents: Bd 2 - Concertino for clarinet, Op. 26

Entries would be made as follows:

Composer entries:
    Weber, Carl Maria von, 1786-1826
        Concerto for clarinet in F Minor, no. 1, Op. 73, by Carl Maria
        von Weber.

    Weber, Carl Maria von, 1786-1826
        Concertino for clarinet, Op. 26 with Concerto for clarinet in
        F Minor, no. 1, Op. 73, by Carl Maria von Weber.

    Weber, Carl Maria von, 1786-1826
        Quintet for clarinet and strings in B flat Major, Op. 34, by Carl
        Maria von Weber.
Added uniform title entry:
    Concertino for clarinet, Op. 26 with Concerto for clarinet in F Minor,
        no. 1, Op. 73, by Carl Maria von Weber.

In these examples, the unifying element is the composer. The next example is like Example 3, except that it includes a work by another composer as well as another work by the composer shown on Side 1 of the phonodisc.

Example 5

Label title:
> BORODIN
> Symphony no. 2 in B Minor
> Side 1
> . . . .
> BORODIN
> In the Steppes of Central Asia
> Side 2
> TCHAIKOVSKY
> Romeo and Juliet

Unit entries:
> Side 1:
> Symphony in B Minor, no. 2, by Alexander Borodin.
> Side 2:
> Symphonic work "In the steppes of central Asia," by Alexander Borodin.

Field Nine:
> Bd. 2 - Symphonic work "Romeo and Juliet," by Peter Ilyitch Tchaikovsky.

Composer entries:
> Tchaikovsky, Peter Ilyitch, 1840-1893
> Symphonic work, "Romeo and Juliet," with Symphony in B Minor, no. 2, by Alexander Borodin.
>
> Borodin, Alexander, 1833-1887
> Symphony in B Minor, no. 2, by Alexander Borodin.
>
> Borodin, Alexander, 1833-1887
> Symphonic works "In the Steppes of Central Asia," by Alexander Borodin.

Title entries:
> Symphonic work: "Romeo and Juliet," by Peter Ilyitch Tchaikovsky with
> Symphonic work "In the Steppes of Central Asia," by Alexander Borodin.

"Romeo and Juliet," by Peter Ilyitch Tchaikovsky with
Symphonic work "In the Steppes of Central Asia," by Alexander
Borodin.

"In the Steppes of Central Asia"
Symphonic work "In the Steppes of Central Asia," by Alexander
Borodin.

There are several things to note about this example. The opus
numbers are omitted because they are not readily available. Schwann
does not supply them as it does the dates and correct spelling of these
composers' names. Romeo and Juliet may be identified by the year
of composition, 1870, but if it is not the practice of the library to
include this as a substitute for opus numbers, then the date of composition may be omitted as well.

The work Romeo and Juliet by Tchaikovsky is on many different
phonodiscs, usually as one side of the item. Cataloged as shown, the
inclusion with works by Borodin would not matter to the user, who
would be able to find the work under the composer's name as well as
the title of the composition. (A very popular song was confected out
of one of the more beautiful melodies in the composition.) When two
different composers each have a different work on the two sides of a
phonodisc, there is no problem at all.

Example 6

Label Title:

D'INDY
Suite in Olden Style for Trumpet Two Flutes and Strings, Op. 24
Side 1

SAINT_SAENS
Septet for Piano, Trumpet, and Strings, Op. 65
Side 2

Unit entry:
Suite for trumpet, two flutes and strings, Op. 24, "In the Olden
Style..." by Vincent D'Indy.
. . . .
Side 1 ....

Composer entries:
D'Indy, Vincent, 1851-1931.
Suite for trumpet, two flutes and strings, Op. 24, "In the Olden
Style..." by Vincent D'Indy.
Saint-Saens, Camille, 1835-1921.
Septet for piano, trumpet, and strings, Op. 65, by Camille
Saint-Saens.

In the next example, there are two ways of cataloging the phonodisc.
It could be considered a collection and cataloged under the title of the
album, or it could be considered three works by three different composers on one phonodisc.

Example 7

Label title:

>   "ITALIAN STYLE"
>   . . . .
>   Side 1
>   (MENDELSSOHN)
>   SYMPHONY NO. 4
>   ("ITALIAN")
>
>   "ITALIAN STYLE"
>   . . . .
>   Side 2
>   (HUGO WOLF)
>   1. ITALIAN SERENADE
>   (TCHAIKOVSKY)
>   2. CAPRICCIO ITALIEN

The problem is what to do with the title of the phonodisc itself.
Otherwise this example is quite similar to Example 6, except that
three composers are included rather than two.

Unit entry:
>   Symphony in A, no. 4, Op. 90, "Italian..." by Felix Mendelssohn.
>   . . . .
>   Side 1
>   . . . .
>   Label title: "Italian Style."
>   Symphonic works "Italian Serande," by Hugo Wolf.
>   . . . .
>   Side 2, Band 1
>   . . . .
>   Label title: "Italian Style"
>   . . . .
>   Bd. 2. - Symphonic work, Op. 45, "Capriccio Italien," by Peter
>   Ilyitch Tchaikovsky.
>   Side 1 - Symphony in A, no. 4, Op. 90, "Italian..."

Cataloged as a phonodisc, the label title "Italian Style" would be
located with the uniform title:

Unit entry:
Symphonic works   "Italian Style."
....
Contents: Side 1 - Symphony in A, no. 4, Op. 90, "Italian" by
Felix Mendelssohn. Side 2 - Bd. 1 - Symphonic work "Italian
Serenade," by Hugo Wolf. Bd. 2 - Symphonic work "Capriccio
Italien," Op. 45, by Peter Ilyitch Tchaikovsky.

Other entries would be the same:

Mendelssohn, Felix, 1809-1847
Symphonic works   "Italian Style."

Wolf, Hugo, 1860-1903
Symphonic works   "Italian Style."

Tchaikovsky, Peter Ilyitch, 1840-1893
Symphonic works   "Italian Style."

However, there is greater clarity and immediacy if the phonodisc is
not considered a collection but rather is cataloged one side at a time.

Composer entries:

Mendelssohn, Felix, 1809-1947
Symphony in A, no. 4, Op. 90, "Italian..." by Felix Mendelssohn.

Wolf, Hugo, 1860-1903.
Symphonic work   "Italian Serenade," by Hugo Wolf.

Tchaikovsky, Peter Ilyitch, 1840-1893
Symphonic work, Op. 45, "Capriccio Italien," with
Symphonic work   "Italian Serenade," by Hugo Wolf.

Where the unifying element is the composer it is best not to treat the
phonodisc as a collection that would be cataloged under the album title
rather than the title of the first individual work on side one. If one
side of a phonodisc is devoted to a single composition, it should be
cataloged following the general rule for entry of single works. Sometimes the album title is essential in identifying a particular collection,
but often enough this is not the case. Especially in phonorecordings of
serious music, the tendency of the producers of phonodiscs is to collect
short works of one kind on a single item, with or without an album
title.

<u>Example 8</u>

Label title:

CHOPIN
ETUDES, OPUS 25
. . . .

Side 1

CHOPIN
ETUDES, OPUS 25
(Concluded)
. . . .

Side 2

TROIS NOUVELLES ETUDES
. . . .
Unit entry:
  Etudes, Op. 25, by Frederic Chopin.
. . . .
  Side 2, Bd. 2, Etudes, "Trois nouvelles etudes"
Composer entries:

  Chopin, Frederic, 1810-1849
  Etudes, Op. 25, by Frederick Chopin.

  Chopin, Frederic, 1810-1849
  Etudes, "Trois nouvelles etudes," with Etudes, Op. 25, by
  Frederic Chopin.

It is not necessary to list all twelve of the etudes published as
Opus 25 because all are included. If a selection had been made, it
would be necessary to list those included with the key indication and
number of each one. This example should be compared with the following:

Example 9

Label title:
  I LIKE TCHAIKOVSKY

. . . .
Side 1

1. POLONAISE FROM
   "EUGENE ONEGIN" (3:52)

2. ARABIAN DANCE FROM
   "NUTCRACKER SUITE"...

3. CHINESE DANCE FROM
   "NUTCRACKER SUITE"...

4. ANDANTE CANTABILE FROM
   "STRING QUARTET NO. 1"...

I LIKE TCHAIKOVSKY

. . . .

Side 2

1. ROMANCE IN F MINOR*...

2. MELODIE*...

3. NONE BUT THE LONELY HEART*...

4. FINALE FROM "CAPRICCIO ITALIEN"...

. . . .

* Arrangements by Carmen Dragon

As can be seen, the unifying elements here are the composer and
the performer even though not listed. The role of the performer as a
unifying element in collections will be considered in the next chapter.
Furthermore, there is no uniformity of type of composition. A portion
of an opera, two selections from a ballet, a movement from a string
quartet, parts of two different symphonic works, and three short
compositions for solo instrument or voice are all put together in one
item. A further problem is found in the three compositions arranged
by Carmen Dragon, who is the conductor of two different orchestras
recorded in this item.

In this example, the title of the collection given by the manufacturer
of the phonorecording serves as a further identifying element. The
inclusion of a wide variety of compositions presents a problem in
selecting a uniform title. The only term that covers this collection is
the word "Selections."

Unit entry:
     Selections   "I like Tchaikovsky" by Peter Ilyitch Tchaikovsky,
          arr. by Carmen Dragon.

The library would decide whether each composition should be noted
in Field Nine and separate entries made for each. If so the following
entries would be made:

Title entries:
     Opera - Selections: Polonaise from "Eugene Onegin" in Selections
     "I Like Tchaikovsky," by Peter Ilyitch Tchaikovsky, arr. by
     Carmen Dragon.

     Ballet - Selections: Arabian dance from "Nutcracker Suite," in
     Selections "I Like Tchaikovsky," by Peter Ilyitch Tchaikovsky,
     arr. by Carmen Dragon.

Ballet - selection: Chinese dance from "Nutcracker Suite," in
Selections "I Like Tchaikovsky," by Peter Ilyitch Tchaikovsky,
arr. by Carmen Dragon.

Quartet for strings - selections: "Andante Cantabile" from Quartet
no. 1, in
Selections "I Like Tchaikovsky," by Peter Ilyitch Tchaikovsky,
arr. by Carmen Dragon.

Symphonic work - selection   Waltz from "Serenade for Strings"
in
Selections "I Like Tchaikovsky," by Peter Ilyitch Tchaikovsky,
arr. by Carmen Dragon.

For the flip side, the compositions would require title entries as
well. Further difficulties would be envountered, seen somewhat in
the title of one of Tchaikovsky's operas, "Evgen Onegin." The label
title gives the spelling as "Eugene Onegin," but the library would have
to settle on the standard conventional title either as transliterated
from Russian, hence "Evgen" or in its French form, hence "Eugène."
Further, the fact that the work has been arranged from another type of
composition must be noted. The unit card, of course, would remain
the same and indication of the unit entry has been omitted in the following examples.

Title entries:
Compositions - arranged   Romance in F Minor,   in...

Compositions - arranged   Melodie   in...

Songs - arranged   Nur wer die Sennsucht kennt (None but the
lonely heart) in

Symphonic works - selections   Finale from Capriccio Italien in...

This kind of music is considered "mood music" by many people who
are accustomed to a musical background furnished in stores, hotel
lobbies, and even factories. There is a question whether the collection
is worth such detailed analysis, especially in view of the selections and
arrangements. Many libraries would be satisfied with only the unit
entry card, a title entry, and an entry for the composer.

Example 10

Label title:
     WALTZ
     CARMEN DRAGON Conductor

There are nine waltzes on this phonodisc, by eight different composers.

Some of these were originally scored for symphony orchestra, such as Sibelius's "Valse Triste," but others, such as Chopin's "Minute Waltz" and "Grande Valse Brilliante," were written for the piano. The conductor has provided the arrangements for these works. This is a collection without the unifying element of composer. Such phonorecordings will be considered in the next chapter.

In the following example, although the phonorecording is not music, the same principles apply.

Example 11

Label title:
    JEAN COCTEAU
    Reads His Poetry and Prose
             Side 1

       Les Voleurs d'Enfants
       Plain-chant
       L'Ange Heurtebise
       Hommage a Manolete
       Un Ami Mort

The flipside of the phonorecording includes four more works by Jean Cocteau. Cataloging this item requires only that the decision about individual works be made in advance. If entries are required for each of the poems and prose selections read by the author, then entry cards will be required for each. Most libraries, however, would find that the users are satisfied with entries that give the author's name and the title of the phonorecording if it differs.

Unit entry:
    Poetry - Selections, "Jean Cocteau Reads his Poetry and Prose."
Unit entry:
    Poetry - selections, by Jean Cocteau.
Author entry:
    Cocteau, Jean,
       Poetry - selections, by Jean Cocteau.

Operas, as noted above, include not only the composer but also the librettist, unless the composer served as his own librettist.

Example 12

Label title:
    . . . .
      "TOSCA"
    (Puccini-Illica & Giacosa)

The procedural manual of a library should indicate how fully information is included for librettists. The three choices are indicated below:

Unit entry:

Opera "Tosca," by Giacomo Puccini.

This omits the librettists altogether. This is, in full-scale cataloging, something less than advisable. If librettists are ever included, they should be always included.

Unit entry:

Opera "Tosca," by Giacomo Puccini: libretto by Ilica and Giacosa.

The following gives sufficient information so that a person interested in the librettists can find them in reference works.

Unit entry:

Opera "Tosca," by Giacomo Puccini: libretto by Luigi Illica and Giuseppe Giacosa.

If entries are made for the librettists, the third choice is the preferable form. The given names of librettists are necessary for entries and including them in the unit card indicates that an entry is to be made for the names. Of the three choices, the first can be employed if the names of librettists are put in Field Eight, Additional Information, and no entries are made for these names. If librettists are considered not significant enough for an entry, then the second choice is preferable.

A similar problem arises with popular songs which may include not only composer and lyricist but also arranger.

Example 13

Label title:

HAPPY HEART
- J. Rae - J. Last -
Arranged by Al Capps
Produced by Jerry Fuller.

The information about the performer is omitted here, although the performer is usually the most important element in a phonorecording of popular music. The question is to what extent does the library wish to make entries for composers, lyricists, producers, and arrangers. The producer is the individual in charge of the phonorecording session and is the first possible omission. The arranger, as noted elsewhere, may also be omitted because of the close connection of arrangers and performers. Even the composer and the lyricist may be omitted, especially in brief-form cataloging. This phonorecording would present some problems because of the lack of given names for composer and lyricist. Such information is much more difficult to locate in reference works, and <u>Schwann</u> does not help much.

Unit entry:
    Popular song "Happy Heart" by J. Rae and J. Last, arr. by
    Al Capps.

This is a complete entry, omitting the producer as insignificant from a musical point of view. Entries would be made for Rae, J and for Last, J   , with considerable space left so that the given names can be supplied when available. So long as there is no entry with an identical name, no harm is done in giving only so much as is customarily included on the label of the phonodisc. If there is another composer or lyricist with the same surname and first initial, then some research is necessary to identify the individuals further.

SUMMARY

Field Two of the description for phonorecordings is used for composers, authors, lyricists, librettists, and arrangers. An entry is made for each of these when the full name, or a usable equivalent, is given.

The above is the rule for entries found in the Second Field of the description. Music libraries ordinarily pay much greater attention to serious music than to popular music, so that information about the creators of a work can be located when needed without excessive difficulty in standard reference tools dealing with music.

Chapter 5

PERFORMERS

Caedmon Records uses an advertising slogan stating that the phonorecording is the third dimension of the printed page. Caedmon
specializes in recorded speech, so that the reason for their advertising
a third dimension is obvious. One of the reasons that the Anglo-
American Cataloging Rules of 1967 are insufficient for cataloging
phonorecordings is that a confusion between the printed score and the
performed music permeates the whole chapter, and the importance of
the performer is never made clear.

Field Three is reserved for performers. This field is equivalent to
the edition field for books. The field may include not only the performers but also the date of the performance if it differs from the date
of the phonorecording. The place of the performance may be included
if that is a necessary part of the identification of the phonorecording.

These are not absolute requirements. Some phonorecordings do not
even specify who the performers are, though these are rare. Some
phonorecordings of octets will give all eight different performers, and
many operas are performed by an orchestra with a conductor and a
chorus with a chorus master, and there may be soloists, other than
singers, especially in the phonorecordings of operas that include
recitative passages usually accompanied on the harpsichord. The
recitative accompanist, the solo performers enacting various roles,
and even other necessary technical personnel, such as the musician in
charge of musical preparation, may be included.

The problem in Field Three, Performers, is to determine how completely the cataloging will reflect what the label title gives. Here the
procedural manual of the library will have to be specific, establishing
rules that limit the inclusion of performers, the conductor and the
principal singers in operas, and conductors and principal soloists for
other music and specifying the names of quartets and other chamber
groups, rather than the names of each member of the group.

A further problem with Field Three, Performers, is that like Field Two, Composer-Creator, this field constitutes the principal means of identification, to the exclusion of title of phonorecording and titles of works performed, not to mention composers of these works. Modern popular music groups, and individuals, often write and sing their own songs, accompanying themselves as well.

Much of the confusion and frustration in the cataloging of phonorecordings arises from the fact that Fields One, Two, and Three are less mutually exclusive than the cataloger might like. There is a definite order of precedence: uniform title, title of composition, title of phonorecording, composer, librettist or lyricist, arranger, and performer (with the principal performers given first). Lacking any of these, the next is used, but the uniform title is never lacking because it is supplied by the cataloger, so that the user can always find the phonorecording he wishes because the cataloger always has a way of making a unit card.

Professional librarians long ago realized that what the cataloger does not do, the reference librarian must. That is, incomplete data on the unit card or insufficient entries will leave the user with questions that the reference librarian must answer. No time is really saved by omitting significant details in the cataloging: it is only spent elsewhere. The user who is too shy to ask questions is the one that librarians worry about. He has gone away dissatisfied without giving any indication of how the catalog failed him.

Music research libraries will need the most complete cataloging with full details on the unit card and many entries for every work cataloged. College libraries that include phonorecordings, and all should because almost all of them do, will require less explicit cataloging. A high school library or a small public library, adequately served by a unique-entry book catalog, can utilize brief-form cataloging. But even here, there may be confusion over how to enter the work, in view of the complexities, which are the same regardless of the kind of cataloging employed.

In computerized systems, Fields One, Two, and Three are searchable fields, so that any name listed here will be available to the user of the system. The manual equivalent is an entry under each of the names listed. There are only two more searchable fields, Field Nine, Contents, and Field Ten, Subject Analysis.

Field Eight is reserved for additional information. Performers for whom no entry is required, although a listing of their names helps to identify the item, can be included in Field Eight. This decision will

rest generally with the professional librarian and should be explained
in a procedural manual. All of the problems of cataloging phonorecordings can be isolated in these five searchable fields. A searchable field
in a computerized system, equally a field for which entries must be
made, is served very well by a unit card system, because cards can
be duplicated rapidly and inexpensively by computer as well as by a
duplicating machine requiring a master. A unique entry incurs the
difficulties of deciding in advance just how the user will look for the
item. Such judgements may be second guessing, at best, perilous in
any case, and more often wrong than right except for small collections.

As in the previous chapters, the problems can be illustrated with
examples. Because of the possibility of confounding composers with
librettists, and lyricists with performers, the recommended practice
is to include the dates of composers, when readily available as in the
Schwann catalog, and the type of instrument used by the performer.
This serves another purpose as well. Sometimes the composer and
the performer are identical. There is great advantage to the student
of music in hearing a work performed by the composer. Usually
these are piano works. (The use of piano rolls made it possible to
record some composers who died before the development of modern
electronic recording techniques.) When the performer and the composer are the same, the entry of the composer as performer is simple
and very informative. The composer's name is given in usual order
with his dates, and the name of the instrument he plays is included.
This is possible only if the performers are always identified by the
instrument they use.

Singers use the human voice as their instrument. Singers of opera
and other serious music have a definite voice range, from soprano, to
mezzo soprano (Italian for middle soprano) to contralto, usually the
voice range of women, to counter tenor or alto, the highest male voice,
to tenor, to baritone, the usual voice range of men, and bass. Popular
singers, so far as some devotees of opera are concerned, simply
squawl in an indeterminate range, when they do not scream unbearably.
For popular singers, many of whom are very accomplished artists,
the voice range is not important. The word "vocalist" is sufficient.
Devotees of popular music do not think of, for instance, Ella Fitzgerald
as a mezzo soprano but as Ella Fitzgerald the vocalist. It would be
very difficult to classify the scratchy voice of the late Louis Armstrong,
and in any case it is unimportant.

Rather than employ such words as "pianist," "violinist," "harpist,"
and "flautist," the name of instrument can be given. Milstein, Nathan;
Violin, as will be seen in the examples below, gives a clear indication

of the performer and the instrument he uses. It serves also to clarify
the type of entry, especially if the composer is also the conductor.
Conductors are indicated with the name of the orchestra they conduct,
then this entry is rotated so that the name of the orchestra comes first
followed by the name of the conductor. A conductor and an orchestra
interact in a way that is not duplicated when the conductor works with a
different orchestra or a particular orchestra is under the leadership of
a different conductor. Similarly, opera companies reflect the musical
talents of the conductor, so that a company is given with the conductor
and the conductor is given with the company.

Example 1

Label title:
                 BEETHOVEN
   SONATA NO. 21 IN C MAJOR
            Op. 53
          ("Waldstein")

     CLAUDIO ARRAU, Piano

Unit entry:
     Sonata for piano in C Major, no. 21, Op. 53, "Waldstein" by
       Ludwig van Beethoven. Perf. by Claudio Arrau.
Conventional title entry:
     "Waldstein"
       Sonata for piano in C Major, no. 21, Op. 53, "Waldstein..." by
       Ludwig van Beethoven. Perf. by Claudio Arrau.
Composer entry:
     Beethoven, Ludwig van, 1770-1827
       Sonata for piano in C Major, no. 21, Op. 53, "Waldstein..." by
       Ludwig van Beethoven. Perf. by Claudio Arrau.

The abbreviation "Perf. by" (for "performed by ") makes the distinction
between composer and performer very clear. In computerized systems
it is a highly usable signal to distinguish between the first two fields
and the third. If it were omitted, a user might think that Claudio
Arrau was an arranger or, if there were such a thing, joint composer.
This example is relatively simple. The succeeding examples demonstrate the complex situations that may be found in the field for performers.

The conventional title for this work, "Waldstein" is actually the name
of the man to whom Beethoven dedicated the sonata, a certain Comte
(Count) de Waldstein, who has vanished into obscurity, remembered
only because a great composer chose to include his name in one of his
most beautiful works for the piano. It would not be fruitful to search

out the complete name of the Comte de Waldstein. A music student
could find the story of the Comte de Waldstein in a biography of
Beethoven, but it is unlikely that the reference librarian would have to
supply this information. If the jacket of the phonorecording is retained
(as it should be) some of the story would appear there.

Example 2

Label title:
    Komponist: Georg Friedrich Händel
    Werk: Feuerwerksmusik   1
                    Orchesterkonzert Nr. 26
            1) Ouverture
    Production: Wolfgang Lohse
    Aufnahme: Alfred Steinke
    Herausgeber: Max Seiffert

           INTERPRETATION

    Berliner Philharmoniker
    Dirigent: Fritz Lehmann

KOMPONIST: Georg Friedrich Händel
WERK: Feuerwerksmusik
    2) Bourree 3) La Paix 4) La rejouissance 5 u. 6) Menuett

PRODUKTION: Wolfgang Lohse
AUFNAHME: Alfred Steinke
HERAUSGEBER: Max Seiffert

       INTERPRETATION

Berliner Philharmoniker
Dirigent: Fritz Lehmann

    This phonorecording was made in Germany and the label is, naturally,
in German. The jacket gives some of the translation. The thing to
be wary of is confusing the personnel in charge of technical aspects of
the phonorecording session with the performers. Fortunately, enough
of the language is similar to English so that the meaning is fairly clear.
Another question is whether the label title of the composition should be
used. Handel's name is spelled in German with a diaresis (two dots)
over the "a" (an umlaut), so that the English spelling would ordinarily
be "Haendel." The library should provide rules that will give a
composer only one spelling of his name. This is especially true of
names transliterated from Russian, or other languages that do not use
the Roman alphabet, and equally an authority list is needed for the

English name of some compositions. Here again the <u>Schwann Record and Tape Guide</u> is essential. The library's supplier of phonorecordings will usually add the monthly issue of <u>Schwann</u> for use in the library sometimes without charge if the order is big enough.

The cataloging of this item should be compared with the transcription of the label title, so that the omission of certain names and such words as "Komponist," "Werk," and "Interpretation" will be understood simply by the names used in the first three fields. The concomitant rule is that labels in foreign languages are reproduced with their English equivalents. This is a departure from the cataloging of books, where the title in the original is important, because a person who does not read the language would be badly served by a catalog entry that leads him to believe the book is in English. However, music is an international language, and the user does not have to know German in order to listen to this music. In point of fact, the music was composed in England, where Handel resided, for a demonstration of fireworks as a part of a celebration ordered by George II, on April 27, 1749, in Green Park, London. The fireworks were a dismal flop, but Handel's music saved the day. The title in Schwann is "Royal Fireworks Music" and that should be used for any phonorecordings that give the title in another language.

Unit entry:
> Symphonic work "Royal Fireworks Music," by Georg Friedrich Handel. Perf. by Berlin Philharmonic cond. by Fritz Lehmann.

Conventional title entry:
> "Royal Fireworks Music"
>> Symphonic work "Royal Fireworks Music," by Georg Friedrich Handel. Perf. by Berlin Philharmonic cond. by Fritz Lehmann.

Composer entry:
> Handel, George Frederick, 1685-1759.
>> Symphonic work "Royal Fireworks Music," by Georg Friedrich Handel. Perf. by Berlin Philharmonic cond. by Fritz Lehmann.

Performer entries:
> Berlin Philharmonic cond. by Fritz Lehmann
>> Symphonic work "Royal Fireworks Music," by Georg Friedrich Handel. Perf. by Berlin Philharmonic cond. by Fritz Lehmann.

> Lehmann, Fritz, cond. Berlin Philharmonic
>> Symphonic work "Royal Fireworks Music," by Georg Friedrich Handel. Perf. by Berlin Philharmonic cond. by Fritz Lehmann.

<u>Schwann</u> gives Handel's name as "George Frederic" in one edition of

its catalog. Some reference books, especially English ones, give the name as George Frederick Handel.

From this much of the unit card, there is little indication that the label title is in German. This becomes quite clear with information about the series and with a note in Field Eight about "Orchesterkonzert no. 26."

Example 3

Label title:

GEORGES AURIC
SUITE FROM "LES MATELOTS" BALLET
(The Sailors)
HOUSTON SYMPHONY ORCHESTRA
EFREM KURTZ, Conductor
(LP 2106)
Solitude: Variations of the Three Sailors

ERIK SATIE
PARADE
(REALISTIC BALLET)
HOUSTON SYMPHONY ORCHESTRA
EFREM KURTZ, Conductor
(LP 2107)
Chorale; Prelude to the Red Curtain;
Chinese Magician; Little American
Girl; Rag-Time; Acrobats; Reprise;
The Red Curtain

This is an old ten-inch Columbia long-playing phonodisc, no longer available. There are many other recordings of "Parade," by Erik Satie, but the Suite from Les Matelots is not listed in a recent issue of Schwann. Cataloging each side as a separate composition reduces the problems of listing contents in Field Nine. Even though the performers are the same, it is good practice to catalog each side separately, as shown below. A further problem is the question of whether Auric's ballet suite should be listed under its French or its English title. If there were many phonorecordings of the ballet suite, a "see" reference would be made from either the French or the English to the title consistently used. Another solution is to put both titles in the catalog, as shown below.

Unit entry:

Ballet suite "Les Matelots," (The Sailors), by Georges Auric.
Perf. by Houston Symphony Orchestra cond. by Efrem Kurtz.

Title entries:
   "Les Matelots" (The Sailors)
   Ballet suite "Les Matelots," (The Sailors), by Georges Auric.
   Perf. by Houston Symphony Orchestra cond. by Efrem Kurtz.

   "The Sailors" (Les Matelots)
   Ballet suite "Les Matelots," (The Sailors), by Georges Auric.
   Perf. by Houston Symphony Orchestra cond. by Efrem Kurtz.
Composer entry:
   Auric, Georges, 1899-
      Ballet suite "Les Matelots," (The Sailors), by Georges Auric.
      Perf. by Houston Symphony Orchestra, cond. by Efrem Kurtz.
Performer entries:
   Houston Symphony Orchestra cond. by Efrem Kurtz
      Ballet suite "Les Matelots," (The Sailors), by Georges Auric.
      Perf. by Houston Symphony Orchestra cond. by Efrem Kurtz.

   Kurtz, Efrem, cond. Houston Symphony Orchestra
      Ballet suite "Les Matelots," (The Sailors), by Georges Auric.
      Perf. by Houston Symphony Orchestra cond. by Efrem Kurtz.
Unit entry:
   Ballet "Parade," by Erik Satie. Perf. by Houston Symphony
   Orchestra cond. by Efrem Kurtz.
Title entry:
   "Parade"
      Ballet "Parade," by Erik Satie. Perf. by Houston Symphony
      Orchestra cond. by Efrem Kurtz.
Composer entry:
   Satie, Erik, 1866-1925.
      Ballet "Parade," by Erik Satie. Perf. by Houston Symphony
      Orchestra cond. by Efrem Kurtz.
Performer entries:
   Houston Symphony Orchestra cond. by Efrem Kurtz
      Ballet "Parade," by Erik Satie. Perf. by Houston Symphony
      Orchestra cond. by Efrem Kurtz.

   Kurtz, Efrem, cond. Houston Symphony Orchestra
      Ballet "Parade," by Erik Satie. Perf. by Houston Symphony
      Orchestra cond. by Efrem Kurtz.

The subtitle "Realistic Ballet" has been omitted in this example,
along with the date of the music, 1917, which might serve in lieu of an
opus number. Note that information about the various sections of the
ballets has not been included here. If the practice of the library is to

include all the information available on the phonodisc, then Field Nine,
Contents, would be the proper place to list the parts of the phonorecording. As mentioned above, the music for a ballet as played by
orchestras in concert rather than at a performance of a ballet may
omit much that the composer wrote. There would be good reason to
include the various sections. Note the difference, as well, in the
uniform titles. The indication is that all of Satie's music for the
ballet "Parade" has been included, while it is quite clear that only a
small section of "Les Matelots" is given on the phonodisc. Note how
many entries are required for a relatively small phonodisc. Libraries
of serious music would require all these entries if the users are not
to be frustrated in their pursuit of information. Even more entries
would be required for phonorecordings that include a soloist as well as
an orchestra.

Example 4

Label title:

Beethoven

CONCERTO No. 2 IN B-FLAT, Op. 19

SIDE 1

First Movement: Allegro con brio

William Kapell, <u>Pianist</u>

NBC Symphony Orchestra

Vladimir Golschmann, Conductor

Beethoven

CONCERTO No. 2 IN B-FLAT, Op. 19

SIDE 2

Band 1 - Second Movement: Adagio

Band 2 - Third Movement: Rondo: Molto Allegro

William Kapell, <u>Pianist</u>

NBC Symphony Orchestra

Vladimir Golschmann, Conductor

   This example practically reproduces the entire label except for information about the producer and the series number. This is an old
ten-inch long-playing phonodisc issued by RCA Victor. William Kapell
was a brilliant young pianist whose sudden death in an airplane accident
was regarded as a major disaster by American musicians. This
phonorecording is not listed in a recent issue of <u>Schwann</u>. A research
library of music would be very glad to have this phonorecording because

the performer built quite a reputation in a very short time. Out-of-print phonorecordings are sometimes re-recorded, and complete cataloging is the only way that the librarian can be certain that the library already has the re-recorded item. Other information may vary considerably. The combination of performers and composition is enough to warn the searcher that the library already owns the original version.

Unit entry:
    Concerto for piano in B flat, no. 2, Op. 19, by Ludwig van
    Beethoven. Perf. by William Kapell, Piano, and NBC Symphony
    Orchestra cond. by Vladimir Golschmann.

Composer entry:
    Beethoven, Ludwig van, 1770-1827
       Concerto for piano in B flat, no. 2, Op. 19, by Ludwig van
       Beethoven. Perf. by William Kapell, Piano, and NBC
       Symphony Orchestra cond. by Vladimir Golschmann.

Performer entries:
    Kapell, William, Piano
       Concerto for piano in B flat, no. 2, Op. 19, by Ludwig van
       Beethoven. Perf. by William Kapell, Piano, and NBC Symphony
       Orchestra cond. by Vladimir Golschman.

    NBC Symphony Orchestra cond. by Vladimir Golschmann.
       Concerto for piano in B flat, no. 2, Op. 19, by Ludwig van
       Beethoven. Perf. by William Kapell, Piano, and NBC Symphony
       Orchestra cond. by Vladimir Golschmann.

    Golschmann, Vladimir, cond. NBC Symphony Orchestra.
       Concerto for piano in B flat, no. 2, Op. 19, by Ludwig van
       Beethoven. Perf. by William Kapell, Piano, and NBC Orchestra
       cond. by Vladimir Golschmann.

In this method of cataloging, there is no question who is the composer, who is the soloist, who is the conductor, and what orchestra participates in the performance.

A problem similar to Example 2 is seen in the following.

Example 5   Side one

Label title: Wolfgang Amadeus Mozart
        Konzert für Violine und Orchester Nr. 5
              A-dur KV 219
       1. Satz: Allegro aperto-Adagio-Allegro
         aperto-2. Satz: Adagio I. Teil
          David Oistrach, Violine
        Sachsische Staatskapelle Dresden
         Dir.: Franz Konwitschny

Side two   16 101 B
Wolfgang Amadeus Mozart
Konzert für Violine und Orchester Nr. 5
A-dur KV 219
2. Satz: Adagio II. Teil - 3. Satz: Tempo di
Menuetto - Allegro - Tempo di Menuetto
David Oistrach, Violine
Sachsische Staatskappelle Dresden
Dir.: Franz Konwitschny

This label in German would be cataloged in English for reasons given
above. No one has to know German in order to listen to Mozart's
great violin concerto, played by a renowned Russian violinist. Supposing
that the cataloger doesn't know German, the problem would be the English
equivalent. Even though this phonodisc is out of print and no longer
available, the concerto is so great that very many different violinists
and symphony orchestras have recorded it. The important facts of
the phonodisc are the names of the individuals in this performance.
The title of the concerto can readily be found in <u>Schwann</u>, the opus
number is a Koechel number for Mozart, used everywhere, and A-dur
translates out as A Major. In American musical practice, because
compositions are either in a minor or a major key, only the minor
key signatures are noted. Major is assumed if it is not stated. The
significant facts of the phonodisc, except for the producer, are all
included here, and these can be found in the Schwann catalog, except
for the English name of the orchestra. The word Sachsische is generally given in English as Saxon. Staatskappelle is roughly State
Chamber Orchestra. It is correct, however, to give the name of an
orchestra in the original language. A very famous orchestra is
L'Orchestre de la Suisse Romande, the Orchestra of the French-
speaking Area of Switzerland, a very awkward and rather inaccurate
translation. Full cataloging is shown for this example, in part as
encouragement because almost all phonodiscs, except those with labels
in Greek, Russian, Chinese, Japanese, or Arabic, should not be regarded as impossible problems. Special collections of folk music may
be found on phonodiscs with as great a variety of languages on the label
as would be expected in book titles. A drama in French, if recorded
in France by a French company, would require that the cataloging be
in French, because the ability of the user to understand the language
would be important. An opera is usually sung in the language of the
country where it is performed. Italian operas are sung in Danish
in Denmark, in German in Austria and Germany, in French in France,
and so on. However, in English-speaking countries the custom is
generally to give the opera in the language of the original libretto, with

some exceptions. Examples below will show how the problem of
language is handled, as an earlier example indicated. For this phonorecording, however, all the German is given in English except for the
proper names.

Unit entry:
    Concerto for violin in A, no. 5, K. 219, by Wolfgang Amadeus
    Mozart. Perf. by David Oistrakh, Violin, and Sachsische
    Staatskapelle, Dresden, cond. by Franz Konwitschny.
Composer entry:
    Mozart, Wolfgang Amadeus, 1756-1791.
       Concerto for violin in A, no. 5, K. 219, by Wolfgang Amadeus
       Mozart. Perf. by David Oistrakh, Violin, and Sachsische
       Staatskapelle, Dresden, cond. by Franz Konwitschny.
Performer entries:
    Oistrakh, David, Violin
       Concerto for violin in A, no. 5, K. 219, by Wolfgang Amadeus
       Mozart. Perf. by David Oistrakh, Violin, and Sachsische
       Staatskapelle, Dresden, cond. by Franz Konwitschny.

    Sachsische Staatskapelle, Dresden, cond. by Franz Konwitschny.
       Concerto for violin in A, no. 5, K. 219, by Wolfgang Amadeus
       Mozart. Perf. by David Oistrakh, Violin, and Sachsische
       Staatskapelle, Dresden, cond. by Franz Konwitschny.

    Konwitschny, Franz, cond. Sachsische Staatskapelle, Dresden.
       Concerto for violin in A, no. 5, K. 219, by Wolfgang Amadeus
       Mozart. Perf. by David Oistrakh, Violin, and Sachsische
       Staatskapelle, Dresden, cond. by Franz Konwitschny.

The next example is also a concerto, already cited in another
example (Example 1, Chapter 4).

Example 6

Label title:

BEETHOVEN
CONCERTO IN C MAJOR FOR
VIOLIN, CELLO, PIANO, AND ORCHESTRA,
Op. 56 ("Triple")

JOHN CORIGLIANO, Violin, LEONARD ROSE, 'Cello,
WALTER HENDL, Piano, with BRUNO WALTER conducting the
PHILHARMONIC SYMPHONY ORCHESTRA OF NEW YORK

This is repeated on both sides of this old ten-inch phonodisc, the
only difference being the movements of the concerto listed on each side.

The usefulness of a unit entry that is easily duplicated can be seen readily in this example. In all cataloging of serious music, the exact spelling of all the names is of critical importance. As in Example 5 of this chapter, the names may be very strange and difficult to spell precisely (Konwitschny, for instance). The unit card system eliminates the possibility of error once the master has been successfully prepared. As each entry is typed onto the duplicated cards, the typist can quickly check to be certain that the spelling is accurate.

Unit entry:
> Concerto for cello, piano and violin, in C,
> Op. 56, "Triple", by Ludwig van Beethoven.
> Perf. by John Corigliano, Violin, Leonard Rose,
> Cello, Walter Hendl, Piano, and New York
> Philharmonic cond. by Bruno Walter.

This is practically complete cataloging of this entry. All that is lacking is the producer, physical description, and series number. The complete unit entry for this phonorecording, also long out of print, would require that an entry be made for each of the performers, for the conventional title "Triple," as well as the composer.

Composer entry:
> Beethoven, Ludwig van, 1770-1827
> > Concerto for cello, piano and violin, in C, Op. 56, "Triple..."
> > by Ludwig van Beethoven. Perf. by John Corigliano, Violin;
> > Leonard Rose, Cello; Walter Hendl, Piano; and New York
> > Philharmonic cond. by Bruno Walter.

Conventional title:
> "Triple"
> > Concerto for cello, piano, and violin in C, Op. 56, "Triple..."
> > by Ludwig van Beethoven. Perf. by John Corigliano, Violin;
> > Leonard Rose, Cello; Walter Hendl, Piano; and New York
> > Philharmonic cond. by Bruno Walter.

Performer entries:
> Corigliano, John, Violin
> > Concerto for cello, piano and violin in C, Op. 56, "Triple..."
> > by Ludwig van Beethoven. Perf. by John Corigliano, Violin;
> > Leonard Rose, Cello; Walter Hendl, Piano; and New York
> > Philharmonic cond. by Bruno Walter.

> Rose, Leonard, Cello
> > Concerto for cello, piano and violin in C, Op. 56, "Triple..."
> > by Ludwig van Beethoven. Perf. by John Corigliano, Violin;
> > Leonard Rose, Cello; Walter Hendl, Piano; and New York
> > Philharmonic cond. by Bruno Walter.

Hendl, Walter, Piano
  Concerto for cello, piano and violin in C, Op. 56, "Triple..."
  by Ludwig van Beethoven. Perf. by John Corigliano, Violin;
  Leonard Rose, Cello; Walter Hendl, Piano; and New York
  Philharmonic cond. by Bruno Walter.

New York Philharmonic Orchestra cond. by Bruno Walter.
  Concerto for cello, piano and violin in C, Op. 56, "Triple..."
  by Ludwig van Beethoven. Perf. by John Corigliano, Violin;
  Leonard Rose, Cello; Walter Hendl, Piano; and New York
  Philharmonic cond. by Bruno Walter.

Note that the word orchestra has been supplied in the entry but omitted in the body of the unit entry. The significant words are New York
and Philharmonic. As with the note about Sachsische Staatskapelle,
Dresden, the name of the orchestra would be established in the catalog
as an authoritative name for the group. This example of multiple
performers of a piece of music is rather rare. Usually there are
fewer names to deal with or more names, and the question is whether
to include all the names if very many are listed.

Example 7

Label title:
                         BRAHMS
                QUARTET NO. 1 IN C MINOR
                      OP. 51, No. 1
                BUDAPEST STRING QUARTET
           (J. Roismann and J. Gorodetzky, Violin;
             B. Kroyt, Viola; M. Schneider, 'Cello)

The question to be resolved in this example is whether all the members of the then Budapest String Quartet should be listed on the catalog
card. Even in libraries that are careful to preserve the jackets in
which phonodiscs are sold, the names may not be easily found, although
a reference librarian in a music library would have little difficulty in
establishing who the performers that comprise an important string
quartet are. String quartets, at least, tend to adopt a name that sometimes outlives the original members who resign or die. Even though
the four members of the Budapest String Quartet are listed, the
cataloger is generally correct in giving only the name of the quartet.
In some music research libraries the actual membership is important
enough to be put on the unit card, although there is not much reason for
making performer entries for each member of the quartet. Field
Eight, Additional Information, is reserved for this kind of additional
detail for which no entries will be made.

Unit entry:
> Quartet for strings in C Minor, Op. 51, no. 1, by Johannes Brahms.
> Perf. by Budapest String Quartet.

Composer entry:
> Brahms, Johannes, 1933-1897
>> Quartet for strings in C Minor, Op. 51, no. 1, by Johannes
>> Brahms. Perf. by Budapest String Quartet.

Performer entry:
> Budapest String Quartet
>> Quartet for strings in C Minor, Op. 51, no. 1, by Johannes
>> Brahms. Perf. by Budapest String Quartet.

The unifying element in each of these examples has been the composer even though a certain orchestra has performed both works, as in Example 3. One further example shows how varied the performer element may be even when the unifying element is the composer.

<u>Example 8</u>

Label title:

SAMUEL BARBER
"KNOXVILLE: SUMMER OF 1915,"
FOR SOPRANO AND ORCHESTRA, Op. 24

ML 2174   FLP 4000

ELEANOR STEBER, Soprano, with
WILLIAM STRICKLAND conducting
THE DUMBARTON OAKS CHAMBER ORCHESTRA

. . . .

SAMUEL BARBER

FOUR EXCURSIONS Op. 20

ML 2174   LP 4406

RUDOLF FIRKUSNY, Piano

Unit entries:
> Symphonic work for soprano and orchestra, "Knoxville:
> Summer of 1915," by Samuel Barber. Text by James Agee.
> Perf. by Eleanor Steber, Soprano, and Dumbarton Oaks
> Chamber Orchestra cond. by William Strickland.
> . . . .
> With Composition for piano, "Four Excursions."

This includes Field Nine, Contents, in order to show that one side of the phonodisc is included in this unit entry.

Composition for piano, "Four Excursions," by Samuel Barber.
Perf. by Rudolf Firkusny, Piano.

Field Nine has been omitted here. It would be similar to the entry for
the flip side.

Composer entries:
Barber, Samuel, 1910-
Symphonic work for soprano and orchestra, "Knoxville: Summer
of 1915," by Samuel Barber. Text by James Agee. Perf. by
Eleanor Steber, Soprano, and Dumbarton Oaks Chamber Orchestra
cond. by William Strickland.

Barber, Samuel, 1910-
Composition for piano, "Four Excursions," by Samuel Barber.
Perf. by Rudolf Firkusny, Piano.
Performer entries:
Steber, Eleanor, Soprano
Symphonic work for soprano and orchestra, "Knoxville: Summer
of 1915," by Samuel Barber. Text by James Agee. Perf. by
Eleanor Steber, Soprano, and Dumbarton Oaks Chamber Orchestra
cond. by William strickland.

Dumbarton Oaks Chamber Orchestra cond. by William Strickland.
Symphonic work for soprano and orchestra, "Knoxville: Summer
of 1915," by Samuel Barber. Text by James Agee. Perf. by
Eleanor Steber, Soprano, and Dumbarton Oaks Orchestra cond.
by William Strickland.

Firkusny, Rudolf, Piano
Composition for piano "Four Excursions," by Samuel Barber.
Perf. by Rudolf Firkusny, Piano.
Entry for author of text:
Agee, James
Symphonic work for soprano and orchestra, "Knoxville: Summer
of 1915," by Samuel Barber. Text by James Agee. Perf. by
Eleanor Steber, Soprano, and Dumbarton Oaks Chamber Orchestra
cond. by William Strickland.

The entry for James Agee is optional. If included in Field Two,
Composer, Lyricist, Librettist, then an entry should be made. This
could be included in Field Eight, in which case, no entry would be made.
Field Eight would be considered additional information; it was taken
from the jacket for this phonorecording. As seen above, the name of
the author of the text sung by the soprano is not included in the information found on the label of this phonodisc.

In the following example, the unifying element is the performer,
Ljuba Welitch, a soprano who made a wildly acclaimed debut at the
Metropolitan Opera in <u>Salome</u> by Richard Strauss. Her performance
of the final scene, the highlight of the one-act opera, has been produced on another label from the one below.

Example 9

Label title:

RICHARD STRAUSS
SALOME - FINAL SCENE

ML 2048   LP 1002

LJUBA WELITCH, Soprano, with
FRITZ REINER conducting the
METROPOLITAN OPERA ORCHESTRA

. . . .
PETER ILYITCH TCHAIKOVSKY
EUGEN ONEGIN -
TATIANA'S LETTER SCENE, Op. 24
(Words by Pushkin)

ML 2048   LP 1003

LJUBA WELITCH, Soprano, and
THE PHILHARMONIA ORCHESTRA
conducted by WALTER SUSSKIND

Even though the performer is the only common element on both sides
of this phonodisc, it cannot be called a collection in the proper sense
of that word. There is only one selection on each side of the phonodisc, and each of these may be cataloged separately. Because of the
complexities of collections, such an example as this is more welcome
than some that will follow. There is not such a difficult problem over
the contents of the phonodisc. In this case, the unit entries have been
made for each of the operas.

Unit entries:

Opera - Selections, "Salome" Final Scene, by Richard Strauss,
Libretto by Hugo von Hofmannstahl after the play by Oscar Wilde.
Perf. by Ljuba Welitch, Soprano, and Metropolitan Opera
Orchestra cond. by Fritz Reiner.

. . . .

Opera - Selections "Eugen Onegin" Tatiana's Letter Scene,
by Peter Ilyitch Tchaikovsky, Libretto derived from
Alexander Pushkin's play. Perf. by Ljuba Welitch and
Philharmonia Orchestra cond. by Walter Susskind.

Full information about the libretti has been included in Field Two. As noted above this could be included in Field Eight, if no entries would be made for the names cited.

In the several examples cited earlier, each shown completely, the function of the unit card in giving all the information for each entry was clearly seen. The entries for the above example would be:

Composer entries:

> Strauss, Richard, 1864-1949
> unit entry

> Tchaikovsky, Peter Ilyitch, 1840-1893
> unit entry

Librettist entries:
> Hofmannstahl, Hugo von, 1874-1929
> unit entry

> Pushkin, Alexander Sergeievich, 1799-1837
> unit entry

> Wilde, Oscar Fingal O'Flahertie Wills, 1854-1900
> unit entry

Performer entries:
> Welitch, Ljuba, Soprano
> Unit entry: Opera - selections "Salome," Final scene ...

> Welitch, Ljuba, Soprano
> Unit entry: Opera - selections "Eugen Onegin,"
> Tatiana's letter scene ...

> Metropolitan Opera Orchestra cond. by Fritz Reiner
> Unit entry

> Reiner, Fritz, cond. Metropolitan Opera Orchestra
> Unit entry

> Philharmonia Orchestra cond. by Walter Susskind
> Unit entry

> Susskind, Walter cond. Philharmonia Orchestra
> Unit entry

In all these examples, the performer has not been the unifying element. Even in the previous example, by cataloging the phonodisc one side at a time, the performer is no longer the unifying element. Collections, however, feature the performer. At times only the performer is of note, as in the following example.

Example 10

Jacket title:
   A Florence   Foster   Jenkins   Recital
Label title:

Mozart
Band 1 - Aria: QUEEN OF THE NIGHT
In German (from "The Magic Flute")

SIDE 1

Band 2 - Liadoff THE MUSICAL SNUFF BOX
In English (English version by Adele Epstein)

Band 3 - McMoon LIKE A BIRD
In English (Words by Mme. Jenkins)

Band 4 - Delibes BELL SONG
In French (from "Lakme")

Band 5 - McMoon SERENATA MEXICANA
In Spanish

Florence Foster Jenkins, Soprano
Cosme McMoon at the Piano
. . . .

David
Band 1 - CHARMANT OISEAU
In French (from "Pearl of Brazil")
with Flute and Piano Accompaniment

SIDE 2

Bach-Pavlovich
Band 2 - BIASSY
In Russian (Based on Prelude XVI by Bach)
(Words by Pushkin)

Johann Strauss, Jr.
Band 3 - ADELE'S LAUGHING SONG
In English (from "Die Fledermaus")
(English version by Lorraine Noel Finley)

Florence Foster Jenkins, Soprano
Cosme McMoon at the Piano

From all appearances on the label, this is a collection of songs
featuring a soprano. The fact that the cataloger has not heard of the
soprano is of no consequence if he believes that the phonorecording
must be completely analyzed so that the user has access to each of the

compositions. This would mean entries for each of the composers, each of the compositions, and possibly for the translators listed on the label, along with entries for the accompanist as a performer and also for the accompanist as composer. The complete unit entry would be long, with Field Nine completely filled with information from the label.

In this case, the jacket is of critical importance, because Florence Foster Jenkins was a musical rarity, a singer who could not sing. She would be forgotten along with many others who attempted to become singers and failed, except that she was wealthy enough to indulge her ambitions. No sensible impresario would have organized and promoted a recital for her, because, in the words of one admirer, "she had a voice like a lawnmower going at top speed." As a society woman of considerable note, she rented space in the old Ritz-Carlton Hotel and cautiously sold tickets to "music lovers," attempting to keep out reporters. Her ultimate triumph, a month before her death, was on October 25, 1944, when Madame Jenkins performed in Carnegie Hall before a capacity audience. Tickets were sold out weeks in advance. To a person who enjoys the great soprano voices that have been preserved in phonorecordings, Madame Jenkins produces sounds that are either incredibly funny or sheer torture.

This lengthy explanation is in part an argument for retaining information printed on the jackets of phonodiscs. The notes by Francis Robinson, at one time assistant manager of the Metropolitan Opera, are amusing and informative. In part, the example shows that many phonorecordings are not what they seem. The user who finds the phonodisc, which has been reissued, unaware of the place of Florence Foster Jenkins in the history of music would be amazed at the sounds he hears. Obviously, complete analysis of this phonodisc would be necessary only in a music research library where students of singing might learn everything they ought not to do from Madame Jenkins's performance.

Unit entry:
     Songs "A Florence Foster Jenkins Recital." Perf. by
     Florence Foster Jenkins, Soprano, and Cosme
     McMoon, Piano.
     . . . .
     Jacket title.

This entry would be used even if Field Nine contained complete analysis of the contents of the phonodisc. The difference in the unit entry is entirely in the degree of analysis decided upon by the policy of the library, and Field Nine, Contents, reflects this policy

completely. Entries made for the contents are not repeated in the last
field, Field Ten, Tracing, because they are listed immediately before
this field. Note that the whole of Field Two, Composer, has been
omitted. The entries in addition to the unit entry would include only
the performers. Whoever played the flute for Madame Jenkins as she
sang David's "Charmant Oiseau" did not gain a place on the label, and
the name would not be included even if considerable research could
locate this information.

Performer entries:

    Jenkins, Florence Foster, Soprano
      Unit entry

    McMoon, Cosme, Piano
      Unit entry

The label title is lacking, but an entry can be made for the jacket
title. However, in this case it seems unnecessary because the name
of the album is the name of the principal performer. The only difference is the order of the names. The rule that the album title is not
given in a separate entry when it is the same as the principal performer
is readily understood by users of a library.

    Opera recordings present the special problem of the number of
performers to include. The following example is a problem only if a
peculiarity of phonorecording companies, and opera programs, is not
understood.

Example 11

REEL ONE

PONCHIELLI

LA GIOCONDA

Cast

La Gioconda, a street singer	ANITA CERQUETTI (Soprano)
La Cieca (the blind woman), her mother	FRANCA SACCHI (Contralto)
Enzo Grimaldi	MARIO DEL MONACO (Tenor)
Alvise Badoero	CESARE SIEPI (Bass)
Laura, his wife	GIULIETTA SIMIONATO (Mezzo-Soprano)
Barnaba	ETTORE BASTIANINI (Baritone)
Zuane	GIORGIO GIORGETTI (Bass)
Isepo	ATHOS CESARINI (Tenor)
A Singer	EDIO PERUZZI (Bass)
A Helmsman	GUIDO PASELLA (Bass)

with The Chorus and Orchestra of the
MAGGIO MUSICALE FIORENTINO

Conducted by GIANANDREA GAVAZZENI

Manufactured by AMPEX

This information is taken from the box containing two reels of
quarter-inch tape. The same phonorecording may be obtained on
discs. This is a reissue of the original phonodisc. Note that the
manufacturer has been included because, just as is the case with books,
the manufacturer (like a publisher) is not the issuer. The organization that prints and binds a book may be mentioned in the front pages
but cataloging does not utilize this information for identification of the
work. In the next chapter problems of manufacturer, producer,
recording company will be resolved rather easily.

The problem here is how many of the characters to list as performers,
in addition to the conductor and the opera company. The orchestra is
usually listed simply as the opera company, unless it is a special
performance of an opera by a symphony orchestra that ordinarily does
not perform such works. In this case, Maggio Musicale Fiorentino is
a special group that performs in May (Maggio) in the city of Florence.
Very many different works are specially produced, of which this opera
is an example. In a library where the librettist is always given, it
will be necessary to look up the opera in any of the numerous reference
works that list it.

The Schwann Record and Tape Guide gives great assistance by listing
the major performers. For this work, under Ponchielli, Amilcare
(1834-1880) La Gioconda (1876), several different phonorecordings are
listed, including Example 11. The listing gives the following names:
Cerquetti, Simionato, Del Monaco, Bastianini, Siepi, Gavazzeni,
Maggio, with the letter "I" in brackets. For operas and other vocal
works the language is given in this fashion. "I" in brackets stands for
Italian. By comparing the listing in Schwann with the information found
on the label of the phonorecording (as shown above), and comparing
this label with information from the jacket, or the container, a good
rule evolves. List the performers noted in Schwann. Note that the
conductor and the orchestra are listed. The Maggio Musicale Fiorentino
is not an opera company but a special orchestra organized for the
music festival.

The cataloging of this opera for a music-research library would be
as follows:

Unit entry:
> Opera "La Gioconda," by Amilcare Ponchielli, libretto
> by Arrigo Boito. Perf. by Maggio Musicale Fiorentino
> cond. by Gianandrea Gavazzeni with Anita Cerquetti,
> Soprano, Mario del Monaco, Tenor, Cesare Siepi, Bass,
> Giulietta Simionato, Mezzo Soprano, Ettore Bastianini,
> Baritone.

Composer entry:
> Ponchielli, Amilcare, 1834-1886
> > Unit Entry

Librettist entry:
> Boito, Arrigo, 1842-1918
> > Unit Entry

Performer entries:
> Maggio Musicale Fiorentino cond. by Gianandrea Gavazzeni
> > Unit Entry

> Gavazzeni, Gianandrea cond. Maggio Musicale Fiorentino
> > Unit Entry

> Cerquetti, Anita, Soprano
> > Unit Entry

> Del Monaco, Mario, Tenor
> > Unit Entry

> Siepi, Cesare, Bass
> > Unit Entry

> Simionato, Giulietta, Mezzo-Soprano
> > Unit Entry

> Bastianini, Ettore, Baritone
> > Unit Entry

If the library wishes to list the other performers, it would use
Field Eight, Additional Information, for the names of singers. In
general, singers who perform the roles of named characters are
listed in Field Three, Performers and unnamed characters indicate
minor roles, so that the singer can be omitted or included in Field
Eight. Sometimes the label and the jacket (or container) will not list
the same characters, omitting the minor roles in one place or the other.

A complete phonorecording of Richard Wagner's tetralogy Der Ring
Des Nibelungen is available on nineteen phonodiscs. There are four
operas, and only the first is relatively short. A very lengthy work
such as this would include very many performers, even if some of

them took several different roles. This is a musical rarity, the work
of one of the greatest composers, and there is also a lengthy explanation
of the work, not to mention several comic phonorecordings, because the
work is not without its possibilities for satire.

Musical comedies, soundtracks, and other works that combine voice
and orchestra may require the listing of a large number of performers.

Example 12

MY
FAIR LADY
Book, Lyrics: ALAN JAY LERNER
Music: FREDERICK LOEWE; Musical Arr.
by ROBERT RUSSELL BENNETT & PHIL LANG
Musical Director, FRANZ ALLERS
REX HARRISON and JULIE ANDREWS with
STANLEY HOLLOWAY, ROBERT COOTE
PHILIPPA BEVANS, MICHAEL KING

OL 4090   SIDE 1

....

1. Overture
"Why Can't the English?" (R. Harrison)
2. "Wouldn't It Be Loverly" (J. Andrews)
3. "With a Little Bit of Luck" (S. Holloway)
4. "I'm an Ordinary Man" (R. Harrison)
5. "Just You Wait" (J. Andrews)
6. "The Rain in Spain" (R. Harrison, J.
Andrews, R. Coote)
7. "I Could Have Danced All Night"
(J. Andrews, P. Bevans)

The flip side of this phonodisc lists the same information except for
the contents of the separate bands. This is a continuation of the
musical portions of this very popular musical comedy. The jacket
gives the names of other performers, including all the members of the
singing ensemble as well as Stanley Holloway's two companions when
he sings "With a Little Bit of Luck." The popularity of this musical
comedy can be judged by the fact that this original cast phonodisc is
available on an eight-track cartridge and both phonodisc and cartridge
are in Schwann. The jacket lists information that would be important
in other fields, for instance the original play by Bernard Shaw,
Pygmalion, from which this musical version was made. It also explains
that the first performance was in New Haven at the Shubert Theatre on
February 4, 1956, and that it opened on Broadway in 1956. It closed
only in 1962, after a long and successful run in New York and London.

The cataloger would find that <u>Schwann</u> does not help with its listing of "Musical Shows, etc." The major performers are not listed. An abbreviation OC in brackets refers to the original cast, but without comparing label and jacket, the cataloger might wonder whether to include Gordon Dilworth, Rod McLennan, Philippa Bevans, and John Michael King. Julie Andrews and Rex Harrison, as the stars, are listed above the title of the musical comedy. The label, in this case, proves to be the better source of information, and gives us the rule to include as major performers only those who clearly have the most important roles, as indicated on the label or the jacket.

The musical director, Franz Allers, is not so important as the conductor of an opera. Although generally accomplished musicians, such men conduct an orchestra organized to present the work rather than a repertory company that presents many different works. There are other problems with such phonorecordings; for instance, is it necessary to list all the arrangers as well as the composers? The following entry will sufficiently identify the work. Note that neither the label nor the jacket calls this an original cast phonorecording. This is sometimes noted on the jacket, or the label, but it is best to leave this designation out if it is not mentioned on the label. <u>Schwann</u> provides the information, with considerable accuracy, if it is needed.

Unit entry:
    Musical comedy "My Fair Lady," by Frederick Loewe, book and lyrics by Alan Jay Lerner, after the play "Pygmalion," by George Bernard Shaw. Perf. by Julie Andrews, Rex Harrison, Stanley Holloway, Robert Coote, and John Michael King, Vocalists.

These are the only performers who have solo parts in the rendition of the score. Philippa Bevans, for instance, is listed only in the selection "I Could Have Danced All Night," and Gordon Dilworth and Rod McLennan are not listed on the label although they are included on the jacket. As noted above and as will be explained in a later chapter, characters and singers, even information about Bernard Shaw and his original play can be given in Field Eight, if desired.

With the listing of performers, the most significant part of the identification of a phonorecording is complete. Brief-listing, or brief-form cataloging, omits all but the most significant details and places the most important element first because this kind of cataloging is ideal for unique entry systems, such as book catalogs or lists of phonorecordings, where only a few are available. One further element is needed for brief-form cataloging, so that with information on the producer, manufacturer, or commercial organization that sells the item, the cataloger is ready to prepare entries for small public libraries, school libraries, and other organizations where the collection of phonorecordings is more a convenience for the user than the basis for serious research in music.

SUMMARY

This chapter introduces the problems to be found in phonorecordings because the performer distinguishes this method of storing information from all others. A phonorecording captures time and holds it prisoner, and as the listener hears the works, he recaptures an original perform-ance, no matter how great a part engineers and other technicians had in its production. The performer is the most significant part of the identification of a phonorecording, so that even brief-form cataloging should include at least the important performers.

No book of rules can account for all possible difficulties in the identification of any source of information, least of all for phonorecord-ings, which constitute a very important source of information storage. The rule for inclusion in Field Three, Performer, is deceptively simple. List all important performers after the abbreviation "Perf. by." This is suggested so that confusion between composers, lyricists, and performers can be avoided. Other examples, because they will deal with information that is not so problematic as Fields One, Two, and Three, will review these three principal means of identification of a phonorecording.

At this point, the reader should feel that he can begin to catalog phonorecordings with some degree of assurance. Usually the beginning cataloger is faced with a situation not covered in the text, such as omission of elements necessary to complete the first three fields of identification, but the rule covering such a case is: "List essential elements as found on the label or other permanent part of the phono-recording." An element that is missing cannot be considered essential. The user, however, may be under the impression that the cataloger has omitted information from carelessness or as the result of an overly restrictive rule governing the amount of identification included in the cataloging. Some libraries will handle this problem by including, possibly in brackets, a note "Perf. unknown." In a computerized system, the programming must take this into account lest a card (or listing) appear under the heading "Unknown Perf." This would be no

great disaster in a music research library.   All the nameless
performers would have their own spot in the alphabetic listing.

The value of the unit-card system in complete cataloging is seen in
the large number of entries required for composer, lyricist, and
performers.   This situation prevails to a lesser extent in books.
When the collections and the necessity of analyzing all the parts of a
phonorecording are considered, making unit entries that serve to
identify a phonorecording helps to resolve some of the confusion that
has attended the cataloging of phonorecordings.   These entries can be
duplicated in as great a number as is necessary, so that relatively
little additional typing will align all the significant points of access in
one alphabetic file, keeping the medium of performance separate from
the form of composition.

Chapter 6

UNSEARCHABLE FIELDS FOR IDENTIFICATION

The next fields to be discussed (Fields Four, Five, Six, Seven, and Eight) are not searchable, because they are used primarily for the purpose of identifying a given phonorecording. The first two of these fields, Four and Five, may even be so similar to Field Seven that the three fields can be condensed into just two fields. Field Six is always included if phonorecordings in more than one form are collected in the library. That is, a library with all its phonorecordings in the form of 12-inch long-playing phonodiscs would have little reason to include information about the form of the recording. A statement that all the phonorecordings are in the same form makes Field Six inconsequential and unnecessary. However, a library that includes phonorecordings in many forms will have to include Field Six in its cataloging. Sometimes this is a crucial element in the identification of the item, especially for those materials reissued in both forms. My Fair Lady is available in cartridge as well as phonodisc form, so that a library with the practice of lending cartridges but not phonodiscs would establish whether the user could borrow the item by distinguishing one form from the other in Field Six.

PHONODISCS

The most common form of phonorecordings is the 12" long-playing (33 1/3 RPM) phonodisc, which may be monaural or stereophonic. This is simply given as

    12" LPM   (Both sides of a 12-inch 33 1/3 monaural phonodisc)
    12" LPS   (Both sides of a 12-inch 33 1/3 stereophonic phonodisc)

If the only variation is the side or the size, the abbreviation LPM, or LPS, can be used for 7-inch, 10-inch, and even 16-inch phonodiscs. The equipment is standardized, so that any turntable that will play one kind of phonodisc will play all kinds.

    1 side 12" LPM   (Complete on one side)
    Side 1, 12" LPM   (Side includes another work)
    3 sides 10" LPM
    Side 1, 7" LPS
    3 sides 16" LPM

A phonodisc with both sides devoted to one composition is shown as above: 12" LPM or 12" LPS.

Note that this kind of phonodisc is only for turntables that will revolve at exactly 100 revolutions in three minutes. The next most common form of phonodisc has a wide hole in the center and revolves 45 times in one minute. A further possibility is the old-fashion 78 RPM (revolutions per minute) phonorecording. These were either 12 or 10 inch, and the oldest among them had a blank side. For speeds other than 33 1/3 RPM, the precise speed must be given:

    Side 1, 7" 45 S   for stereophonic phonorecordings
    1 side 7" 45 M   for monaural phonorecordings

Because all 78 RPM phonorecordings are monaural, there is no need to distinguish between the items in this form. The abbreviation RPM may be used, the distinction between compositions on one side of a phonorecording and those on both sides preserved, and the size given. The size is often an important indication of the storage used for the phonorecording. It is wasteful of space to store phonorecordings of all different sizes mixed together. The phonorecordings should be sorted out by size and each stored separately.

    4 sides 12" 78 RPM

Sometimes complete operas were made available on 78 RPM phonodiscs. The number of sides is counted, even though there may be 18 or 20 sides for one complete work. As emphasized in previous chapters, the minimum of physical form to be cataloged is one side. A composition complete on one side of a phonodisc is so designated, along with other compositions that may be on more than two sides. A composition on both sides of a single phonodisc omits all but the indication of size and speed. For instance, the phonorecording of Wagner's opera Tristan and Isolde is on five long-playing phonodiscs. The physical description of this set would be

    10 sides 12" LPM

The composition is the deciding factor in the use of Field Six. A collection of works on both sides of a phonodisc is shown as 12" LPS, if in stereophonic sound. Libraries collecting the new quadrophonic phonorecordings can use the abbreviation LPQ, which indicates that four-channel decoding is necessary to reproduce the sound. This may be unimportant if the listener must use headphones to hear the phono-recording. So far, two ears seem to be the maximum for everyone. LPQ might indicate a phonorecording that will be played in a special listening room. LPS and LPM are rather more standardized as abbreviations than other possibilities.

PHONOTAPES

Reel-to-reel tapes may be of various sizes, although the 7" reel is fairly standard. They may be monaural, stereophonic, and quadra-phonic. The speed may vary from 1 7/8 ips, (inches per second) to 15 ips. The most common for music are 3 3/4 and 7 1/2 ips. A library in a country where the metric system is commonplace may want to show these speeds in centimeters per second, 9.5 cps, 19 cps, 38 cps. The least speed would be 4.75 cps, suitable only for the recording of speech.

Reels may have up to four separate channels, called tracks; two tracks are ordinarily taken up on side of the reel, so positioned that the remaining tracks are separate and backwards. The actual tracks would be side 1 track 1, side 2 track 2, side 1 track 3, and side 2 track 4. These tracks are used in pairs for stereophonic recordings so that the tape may be turned over to one side or the other for a given part of a phonorecording. Strictly speaking, of course, the side is inconsequential except as it shows the direction the tape should be played. Tape decks with reversing mechanisms do not require that the tape be turned over and fitted onto the sprockets again. The word side, however, will still be meaningful because the tracks on side 1 means that the tape will be unwound from the outer edge and be moved to the empty reel at the left. Side 2 would indicate the reverse; an empty reel taking uptake at the right of the full reel. Remember that in facing the tape deck, you are looking at a kind of mirror, your right hand is the tape deck's left, and vice versa. To prevent confusion over which way the tracks run, they may be designated side 1, or side 2.

7" Reel   1 7/8 ips S   Reel at the slowest speed, stereophonic
7" Reel   1 7/8 ips M   Reel at the slowest speed, monaural
7" Reel   3 3/4 ips S   Reel at the common speed, stereophonic
7" Reel   3 3/4 ips M   Reel at the common speed, monaural
7" Reel   7 1/2 ips M or S   Reel at the fast speed, monaural or
   stereophonic

Where sides or tracks are important they must be indicated : 7" Reel 7 1/2 ips 2 track S would indicate two-track stereophonic recording. Note that the physical description includes only the variation from a standard. Because the speeds are highly standardized, and only four are used, the abbreviations SP for slow speed, CP for common speed, and FP for fast speed, with HP reserved for 15 ips, would give a kind of code for reels. If all the reels are 7", there is no need to account for the size. If the reels vary only between 3", 5", 7", then there is reason to show the variation. If both sides, all four tracks, are always used, then there is no need to show a variation for the side or the track. Either may be used, tracks 1 and 3, representing side 1, tracks 2 and 4, representing side 3. Track 1S would indicate a stereophonic recording using the paired tracks 1 and 3. Track 2S would indicate the other paired tracks. The equipment used by the library fairly well determines what the rules of physical description would be.

Reel SPM Tr 1   The reel of tape at slow speed, monaural, using
                 only the first track.

Reel SPM Tr 2   The same but using track 2.

All prerecorded tapes are on 7-inch reels, usually stereophonic. Only the first such tapes were two-track. The present practice is to use all four tracks. Reel-to-reel tape recording has been replaced to a great extent by cartridges and cassettes. The reels are highly subject to damage; so the best practice is not to lend the reels and to play the tapes only on a deck that lacks recording facilities. An absent-minded attendant who pushes the record and play buttons at the same time can wipe out a prerecorded selection. These are much more expensive than phonorecordings in any other form. The tapes are long-lasting but subject to breakage. If stored in a hot dry place, they may become very brittle.

CARTRIDGES AND CASSETTES

Because tapes in this prepackaged form are of standard size and speed, the only variation is between monaural and stereophonic, or quadraphonic for cartridges. Special recording equipment is needed for each kind. The cassette tape recorder is so inexpensive that some libraries lend both the recorder (capable only of playing cassettes) and the cassettes. Cassettes are subject to damage by re-recording as well as accidents that occur, such as the eighth-inch tape becoming wound around the guide post in the recorder or coming loose from the winding posts on either side. They can be repaired by anyone with a small screwdriver, patience, and a steady hand. The physical description does not need to take into account the question of size or speed.

Cartridge, 4-channel stereophonic, may be abbreviated to Cartridge 4CS, and if all the cassettes are monaural, rather more common than stereophonic cassettes and players, which are much more expensive than the monaural kind, then the word cassette is sufficient description for material in this form. Commercially prerecorded cassettes are usually stereophonic. Sometimes the side of the cassette is important, and if so it may be indicated along with the length of time the cassette plays. This is counted as a whole, not for each side, so that a 15 minute cassette plays for 7 1/2 minutes on each side. This is the shortest playing time, hence least amount of magnetic tape, that can be found in a cassette. The times increase as multiples of 15 minutes per side from 30 minutes, 60 minutes, 90 minutes to 120 minutes. The last is the largest size cassette, in that it contains more tape than any of the others, so much that there is greatest risk of accidents with 120-minute cassettes. Ninety-minute cassettes are the longest safe-playing ones.

    Cartridge 4 CS
    Cassette 15'
    Cassette 30'
    Cassette 60'

Commercially recorded cartridges are more common than cassettes, although both have become major enterprises recently. Note that the whole cartridge or whole cassette is described in Field Six. The individual parts of the cassette, or the reel or cartridge, are indicated in Field Nine, Contents. If there are four programs on a cartridge, providing that the uniform title and cartridge title apply to all the contents, then one entry is needed for the cartridge with details included in Field Nine.

In the examples that have preceded, in those that follow, and especially in the examples at hand, the reader can see how the physical description included in Field Six is determined for each item in a collection. The collection as a whole must be considered, then the peculiarities of the four most common forms of phonorecordings. Special problems, such as historical collections of cylinders or movie soundtracks, deserve special consideration. A movie soundtrack in the original form of light signals on film, if separate from the movie itself, can be indicated with a little practical work.

The rule to keep in mind, and one that makes standardization difficult in phonorecordings, is that no more should be noted than is necessary. If precataloged tapes become available, then the standardization will have to take into account all the variety of phonorecordings that may exist in a library.

The most common use of a cassette is for locally produced phonorecordings. The running time of the cassette becomes important then. Most commercial prerecorded cassettes do not specify the time, nor is there any need to do so in Field Six, Physical Description. If there are several selections these may be indicated in Field Nine, Contents, with the time of the selection if that is important.

In order to preserve the delicate surface of phonodiscs, many libraries copy the contents of separate bands onto cassettes for easy playing. This saves damage to the phonorecording. Probably companies that prepare the phonodisc are not too happy about this practice, but so long as a library does not charge admission fees for its recorded concerts or the use of its cassettes, there is nothing illegal about the practice. The physical description would be the only variation in the cataloging of a phonodisc a part of which has been copied onto a cassette. Each part would be separately cataloged and Field Six, Physical Description, would make it clear that the work is available in cassette form.

Special turntables now available that will mechanically set the needle down on the phonodisc partially resolve the problem, but they are more expensive than other turntables. So far, the re-recording of bands or cuts in a phonodisc so that the user can borrow the cassette rather than mangle the tracking of the phonodisc seems to be the most practical way of making individual selections in a collection of works available to the public. Both cassettes and cartridges represent special custodial problems because they are very easily concealed on the person of a predatory user of the library. They should not be put in the open, but they should be available to the borrowers of a library by asking at a service desk. Theft of library materials remains an irritating and frustrating problem, and the cassette collection on open racks is subject

to rapid loss. As the problem of theft grows, libraries must take
steps to remove temptation.

PRODUCER, LABEL IDENTIFICATION NUMBER, PRODUCER'S SERIES NUMBER

Fields Four, Five, and Seven are used to identify the producer, the
item and the series of which the item is a part. Because the guiding
rule for all cataloging of phonorecordings is to prevent duplication of
information, these fields represent the clearest options for the
cataloger. Field Four is used for the producer or distributor of a
phonorecording. The Schwann catalog lists seven double-column
pages of producers of phonodiscs and phonotapes, and includes the
prices, the series numbers that are related to prices, and the web
of interrelated label titles emanating from one producer.

A library that makes phonorecordings must add another producer,
the library itself. Because Field Seven, Producer's Series Number,
requires both the producer and the series number, this field may be
used for commercial phonorecordings; Fields Four and Five would be
reserved for locally produced phonorecordings and the date the recording was completed. Then the series number and the producer's label
name will suffice to identify almost all phonorecordings. If the library
does not make phonorecordings, or at least none that is added to the
collection, then the producer's name and series number may be placed
in Fields Four and Five. Field Seven is then omitted entirely for all
phonorecordings.

Because a producer is very like a publisher, the practice usually
adopted by book catalogers is to prefer Field Four and Five and to use
Field Seven not for the ordinary series number but for a very special
one. Field Four is not so difficult to manage as may appear. The
name of the producer as it appears on the label (in preference to the
manufacturer) is given as found: Columbia; RCA Victor; Turnabout;
Angel; Everest, etc. Such words as Records, Recording Company,
that only complete the identification of the producer are omitted.
Angel Records is not more distinct than Angel. Such words as
Masterworks Series, Red Seal, are omitted because these are series
indication. Abbreviations are accepted only if they appear on the label.
The jacket may show AF Living Stereo, but the label of the phonodisc
specifies Audio Fidelity 1st Component Series. Audio Fidelity would
be included in Field Four. Alshire Records Presents would be

shortened to Alshire, because the other words are not needed for identification. The Schwann catalog can be checked and the producer as listed there in boldface type can be used in Field Four. The lightface type and references to the parent company should be ignored. The Schwann catalog is primarily a buying guide and the indication of price is more important for the acquisitions librarian than for the cataloger.

Field Five is reserved for the item number, as distinct from the series number. This is sometimes stamped or etched into the plastic of a phonorecording. Sometimes it is repeated on the label; sometimes it is the same as the series number. All possible variations exist. The item number is the only means of completely identifying a given phonodisc, made at a certain time. If the label is damaged or destroyed so that the information is unreadable, the item number will provide a means of identification. This would be extremely hard to check because Fields Four and Five are ordinarily unsearchable. No added entries are made in a manual system for producer or item number. The practice of commercial phonorecording companies is not consistent, even within the same company, let alone throughout the industry. The library must adjust to the realities of the phonorecording industry rather than expect the opposite to occur. Phonorecording companies will not change to suit the preferences of catalogers.

In view of these distinctions, there are three options for the librarian. The policy should be established in advance of any cataloging and remain unchanged. Hence, the decision is important. First, the producer's name and the item number can be included in Fields Four and Five. The information on the series can be given in Field Seven. For this option, complete description is exemplified below:

Example 1

Label:

COLUMBIA
MASTERWORKS
MY
FAIR LADY
Book, Lyrics: ALAN JAY LERNER
Music: FREDERICK LOEWE; Musical Arr.
by ROBERT RUSSELL BENNET & PHIL LANG
Musical Director, FRANZ ALLERS
REX HARRISON and JULIE ANDREWS with
STANLEY HOLLOWAY, ROBERT COOTE,
. . . .

OL 5090   Side 1
Nonbreakable   (x "LP" 37804)
. . . .
(on unrecorded space beyond the label: XLP 37804)

(Option 1) Unit entry:

> Musical comedy "My Fair Lady," by Frederick Loewe,
> book and lyrics by Alan Jay Lerner. Perf. by Rex Harrison,
> Julie Andrews, Stanley Holloway, Robert Coote, Vocalists.
> Columbia XLP 37804.
> 12" LPM (Masterworks OL 5090)

This kind of cataloging is complete for all the identifiable and
important features of the phonodisc. The second option would omit
the phonodisc item number and substitute the series number.

(Option 2) Unit entry:

> Musical comedy "My Fair Lady," by Frederick Loewe,
> book and lyrics by Alan Jay Lerner. Perf. by Rex Harrison,
> Julie Andrews, Stanley Holloway, Robert Coote, Vocalists.
> Columbia Masterworks OL 5090
> 12" LPM

The third option would include the series information in Field Seven,
both producer and item number, omitting them from Fields Four and
Five. Note that the only significant change is inclusion of "Columbia"
in the series information.

(Option 3) Unit entry:

> Musical comedy <u>My Fair Lady</u>, by Frederick Loewe,
> book and lyrics by Alan Jay Lerner. Perf. by Rex Harrison,
> Julie Andrews, Stanley Holloway, Robert Coote, Vocalists.
> 12" LPM (Columbia Masterworks OL 5090)

Note that Field Six, Physical Description, does not include mention
of the number of sides, it being assumed that unless the sides are
noted there are always two sides of a single phonodisc.

Example 2

Label title

RCA VICTOR

LM   Side 1
6008-1 In Italian

Verdi Il Trovatore
. . . .

Nicola Moscona, Bass, Margaret Roggero, Mezzo-soprano,
Zinka Milanov, Soprano, Leonard Warren, Baritone,
Jussi Bjoerling, Tenor, Fedora Barbieri, Mezzo-soprano
The Robert Shaw Chorale
Robert Shaw, Conductor
RCA Victor Orchestra
Renato Cellini, Conductor

LONG 33 1/3 PLAY

This is the label for the first phonodisc. There is another phonodisc,
so that the complete opera is presented on four sides of two phonodiscs
in sequence for automatic changers, that is side 4 is the flipside of
side 1, and side 3 is the flipside of side 2. On the blank space just
beyond the label is the phonodisc item number, E2 RP 4107-9S. This
is repeated on each phonodisc with the additional numbers A1, A2, A3,
or A4, according to the side of the phonodisc. Note that the label does
not give the names of the librettists (Salvatore Cammarano and Luigi
Bardare, after the play by Gutierrez).

This phonorecording provides an example of the remaining unsearchable
field, Field Eight, Additional Description. Many libraries find that
information is necessary to complete the identification of the phonorecording or assist the reference librarian in the answering of questions
that users have. While this information is useful, it need not be made
a point of access. A good example is the librettists, or lyricists as in
the example above. In the unit entry reproduced below, the names of
the librettists are put here. Additional information of all kinds can be
included in this field, but in a computerized system it is not searchable
and must be duplicated in the tracing if it is to be made searchable. In
a manual system the rules would specify that information included in
Field Eight, Additional Description, should not be the source of entries.

Unit entry:
Opera Il Trovatore, by Guiseppe Verdi. Perf. by Renato Cellini
cond. RCA Victor Orchestra; Robert Shaw cond. Robert Shaw
Chorale, with Zinka Milanov, Soprano, Leonard Warren, Baritone,
Jussi Bjoerling, Tenor, and Fedora Barbieri, Mezzo-Soprano.
RCA Victor, LM 6008-1, -2, -3, -4.
4 sides 12" LPS Boxed, Automatic sequence.
Includes Libretto by Cammarano and Bardare after the play by
Gutierrez.

In this entry, all the searchable and unsearchable fields deriving from
the phonodisc itself have been included. Note that the performers have
been rearranged and two singers have been omitted. First the conductor

of the orchestra and the conductor of the chorale group, then the
principal singers. From the program in the libretto one can see that
the four names cited are the leading characters: Manrico (tenor),
Leonora (soprano), Count de Luna (baritone), and Azucena (mezzo-
soprano). Furthermore, the box in which the phonodiscs are kept
includes only the names given in the above entry. The label number
rather than the item number incised into the blank space beyond the
label, is used to identify the set. This with the producer is sufficient
for identification. The number of sides and the optional information
about the sequence of sides is included with physical description, but
there is no series information. Because the libretto is furnished
with the phonorecording, this is noted in Field Eight, Additional
Description.

Field Eight can also include notes about the phonorecording. Sometimes labels are reversed and side 1 gets put on the phonorecording for
another side; sometimes the labels are wrong. The correct labeling
should be supposed, if it does not exist, in Fields One, Two, Three,
Four, Five, and Seven. Field Eight, Additional Description, can
explain the variance between the catalog and the label. The note for
a work that is contained on one side of a phonodisc for which cataloging
of another complete work is put in Field Eight. With _____,
Side _____. This is unsearchable because the work is separately
cataloged.

Some phonorecordings are damaged in one spot or another. This can
be noted in Field Eight, Additional Description. Some famous phonorecordings made at an earlier time, before the development of
stereophonic sound, have been re-recorded with technical rearrange-
ments that very nearly duplicate the sound of stereo. This can be
explained in Field Eight, including reissues of old phonorecordings of
all kinds. When the title is taken from the jacket this is noted in
Field Eight.

With the completion of Field Eight, all the fields necessary for brief-
listing or brief-form cataloging have been explained. The field that is
most subject to variation, therefore most difficult, is Field One, Title.
Because this field is the principal means for identifying phonorecordings
and for searching for phonorecordings, the examples throughout have
emphasized the variations in labeling that are found in commercially
produced phonorecordings. In brief-form cataloging, the most significant element is placed first, followed by the information from various
fields. Only the first item is out of order; all the other fields are
shown in the sequences explained above. Any field may be omitted,
but the fields may not be rearranged.

Obviously the most important element will be found in one of the searchable fields, One, Two, and Three, and not in the unsearchable fields, Four, Five, Six, and Seven. Information for the user may be severely limited.

At this point it is necessary to review the eight fields discussed so far. The two remaining fields are reserved for searchable information. Field Nine, Contents, is used for those phonorecordings that contain more than one work on each side of a phonorecording, what have been called Collections. This field is not duplicated in the tracing, because every item is searchable. In an adequately programmed computerized system, Field Nine is the last to be used. Entries are available directly from the contents of any field, but especially Fields One, Two, and Three. In a manual system, Field Ten is used to list the various access entries that will be made for the catalog. In the following summary of the eight fields, an indication is made about the entries that will be required. A computer programmer and a librarian who plan to put their cataloging into a computerized system can follow this analysis of information to be found on labels of phonorecordings in developing the system.

Whatever the system, accuracy in transcribing information from the label of a phonorecording is essential. The names are strange, derived from several different languages, and the cataloger unfamiliar with them must check and recheck his work. The catalog is prepared for the future, so far as both the user and the library are concerned. A catalog must be hospitable to new items as they are received in a library. It is much more than inventory because it provides access to the information contained on phonorecordings. Mistakes in spelling cannot be tolerated. The user, if he knows the name he is searching for, will look in the right place, but he will not find what he is looking for. The computer cannot judge spelling. It accepts whatever is input, and if the user's inquiry is correct, he will be misled by the computer than can only accept what is input as correct.

SUMMARY OF IDENTIFYING FIELDS

Field One: Title, Searchable, Principal Field.

Kinds of Titles

Uniform title: Derived from a list used for all phonorecordings, based on the form of the composition (opera, symphony, sonata, quartet, concerto, etc.) Includes in this order Instrument if variable, as in sonatas, quartets, concertos; omitted if the form indicates the kind of instrumentation required; for instance, opera, symphony, ballet suites, etc. If different instrumentation is used, this would be noted.

Principal key follows instrument. This is given wherever necessary to identify the work. It would be omitted from works where it is variable or does not aid in identification, as in operas, ballets, and other works with a fixed conventional title.

Opus number or its equivalent follows the musical key. The uniform title consists of form, instrument, principal key, opus number or equivalent.

Conventional title: A title given to the work by the composer or by others. If the uniform title is one word, as in the case of operas, the conventional title may come immediately after the uniform title.

Alternate conventional title: This always includes the word or. If the alternate conventional title has fallen into disuse, it is not included. Gilbert and Sullivan operettas commonly included an alternate title now forgotten.

Label title: The title of a work as found on the label of a phonorecording. It may be in agreement with the uniform title and the conventional title, or it may be quite different. It may be the same as the title found on the jacket, or it may differ. The label title is always used for collections of works, if available.

Jacket title: The title of a work as found on the outer covering of the phonorecording. The label title is preferred to the jacket title, because the latter may more easily be lost or destroyed. If the label title is lacking, then the jacket title is used.

Assigned title: A locally produced phonorecording that lacks any title whatever may be given a title by the librarian. This is an assigned title. It should be fixed onto the work itself. The assigned title is used only if the work has no title. If a collection of works is made, then the title of the first work is used to identify the phonorecordings.

Field Two, Composer, Creator, Librettist, etc. Searchable

The individual or individuals responsible for the informational content of a phonorecording are listed in Field Two. A composer is listed first, a librettist or lyricist immediately afterwards, and an arranger after both of these. Arrangers may include composers who complete

a work left unfinished by the original composer; for instance, Franco
Alfano, who completed Turandot after Giacomo Puccini had died of a
heart attack, following an operation for cancer of the throat. Arrangers,
such as Richard Russell Bennett, who has provided the orchestration
for many different musical comedies, would be included after the
composer and the librettist. If there are joint composers, joint librettists, and arrangers, so that the field is unusually full of names, some
of these may be listed in Field Eight. If the library generally omits
the name of the librettist, then librettists and arrangers can be listed
in Field Eight, Additional Description, when necessary. Care should
be taken that some compositions better known for the arrangement
than for the original can be adequately cataloged; the Bach-Gounod
"Ave Maria," for example.

The author of spoken works is included in this field, but producers,
technicians and others are not included here. If necessary for identification, producers of phonorecordings or the technicians who assist
in their preparation can be included in Field Three, Performer, or
Field Eight, Additional Description. The producer is much like the
conductor of an opera, and inclusion in Field Three would necessitate
an access entry to the name. If no such access is needed, then the
names can be included in Field Eight, Additional Description, where
the process of identification is furthered, but access entries are not
made.

Field Three, Performers. Searchable.

All the important performers are listed in this field, always beginning with the conductor and the orchestra if named on the label or the
jacket. Other soloists are included up to the limit advisable for the
entry. Minor characters in operas, instrumentalists who play brief
obbligati, and the members of a small group, even though named on
the label or the jacket, are omitted from the body of the entry (Fields
One through Five). If necessary for the purpose of identification,
minor characters, instrumentalists, etc. can be included in Field
Eight.

The abbreviation "Perf. by" introduces the field, and the conductor
may be listed first with the abbreviation "cond." between the name of
the conductor and the orchestra or group he conducts. Each of the
important soloists is named with the voice range for singers of serious
music or the word "vocalists" for singers of popular music, or the
name of the instrument that an instrumentalist plays.

If the date of the performance is important for the purposes of identification of the phonorecording, it may be included here provided it differs from the date of the phonorecording. If the date the phono- recording was made is the same as the date of the performance, this information is included in Field Five.

If the title of the phonorecording is the name of the performer, the performer may be omitted from Field Three. Accompanists and orchestras with conductors are included in Field Three if named on the label and the same for all the selections. If several names are given, they may be omitted if different for each selection. The ab- breviation "Perf. with" may be used in place of "Perf. by." If the name of the performer differs from that established in the catalog, then the name must be given again in the correct form in Field Three, along with accompanists. The proper word for the voice range of the singer, or the designation "vocalists", must be included in Field One, Title, if the name of the performer is given there and not included in the title.

Field Four, Producer, Distributor. Unsearchable.

The name of the company that produces the phonorecording may be given in this field or in Field Seven, Producer's Series. Locally produced phonorecordings are always given in this field with the words "Locally recorded." The producer or distributor may differ from the manufacturer. The purpose of the field is to notify the user where he can obtain another copy or who distributed the phonorecording. The manufacturer is of secondary significance. However, if the producer has many different series, a common enough occurrence in the phono- recording industry, the producer is given in Field Four and the series name and number in Field Seven. Technicians who are important for purposes of identification may be included here or in Field Eight, Additional Description. At times the producer is an individual who is named on the label. If the producer is a separate individual and the distributor is also named, both the producer's name and the distributor are listed here, with the producer's name given first, Prod. by Name Name for Blank Company.

Field Five, Identifying Number. Unsearchable.

This field is reserved either for the date of recording for locally produced phonorecordings or for the number that identifies the item, as distinct from the number that identifies the item within a series. If the number is the same for both, Field Seven may be preferred. Both fields Four and Five may be omitted if the series identifying

number is sufficient. It is often very difficult to ascertain the date of
a commercial phonorecording.

Field Six, Physical Description. Unsearchable.

The kind of phonorecording is limited to relatively few possibilities,
except in historical collections. Phonodiscs may be different sizes
and speeds, but the most common type is 12 inch, 33 1/3 RPM 'long-
playing.' In specifying the kind of phonorecording, the number of
sides cataloged is indicated first, except when both sides of a single
phonodisc contain one composition, or a composition that occupies
most of both sides with another limited to a section of one side. After
the side comes the size of the phonodisc, then the speed, indicated either
by the exact speed, 16, 45, 78 RPM, or, if 33 1/3 RPM, by the abbreviation LP, with S or M added to indicate stereophonic or monaural phonorecordings. Cassettes, Cartridges, and Reels are indicated by these
words. Reels must include both the size and the speed, which may vary
from 1 7/8 inches per second to 15 inches per second. The abbreviation
S, for stereophonic, or M, for monaural, can be used with cassettes
and reels. Almost all cartridges are stereophonic, utilizing four
different tracks.

Field Seven, Distributor's Series Number. Unsearchable.

This field is used when the producer or distributor utilizes two
different numbers, one to indicate the item uniquely and one to indicate
the series to which the item belongs. Some phonorecording companies
use many different names to indicate the kind of phonorecording; for
instance, Angel re-records compositions and includes them in a series
named Seraphim. Where it is important to distinguish between the
parent company and the series lable, Field Seven may be utilized.
Many libraries do not need such careful identification and may use
either Fields Four and Five, or Field Seven. If the latter is preferred,
Fields Four and Five can be reserved for locally produced phonorecordings.

Field Eight,   Additional Description. Unsearchable.

This field is used for identifying features that are not to be included
as access entries: the librettists of operas, the arrangers of music,
lyricists, the original work from which the item was derived. If the
identifying feature is to be made an access entry it should be included
in Fields Two or Three. This field can be omitted except for notes

about the condition of phonorecordings. When the surface of a phonodisc is damaged a note can be included in Field Eight, Additional
Description. Another necessary note is included in this field to
account for the mislabeling of a phonodisc, not too rare an occurrence.

These represent all the fields needed for brief-form listing. As can
be seen, there is considerable freedom in the unsearchable fields.
Under certain circumstances all of them may be omitted, although it
is generally wise to include Field Six and Field Seven when phonorecordings of several kinds, speeds, and sizes are in the collection.
A knowledge of the possible sources of information and the value of
each to the cataloger will enable the library technical assistant to
prepare a brief-listing, usually sufficient for a small public or school
library.

The procedure is to take the most important element and list it first.
This may be the title of the phonorecording as found on the label or the
jacket, especially if a collection of works by various composers
performed by different artists constitutes the item to be cataloged.
Another possibility is the composer, especially for serious music. If
a relatively limited number of composers are included in the collection
then the composer's name may be shortened so that the first name and
dates are not used unless necessary to distinguish between two composers. Finally, and most commonly for popular music, the performer
may be listed first in the order that is most distinct for the cataloger.

Chapter 9 is a catalog of phonorecordings with an index arranged as
examples of brief-form entries. Brief-form cataloging is a unique-
entry system, that is, only one entry is made for each item. If many
different entries are needed, then the title unit entry system is
recommended as not only the fastest and most distinct, but also the
easiest to utilize. This system assumes some rapid means of
duplication, so that the unit entry is reproduced as often as necessary
to provide detail for each of the access entries required. This can
be quite a number of cards, especially for collections requiring complete analysis, the subject of the next chapter.

Chapter 7

ACCESS FIELDS

The last two fields are reserved for information that will be made into entries in a manual system or that are completely searchable in a computerized system. These fields are especially important for a common type of phonorecording, a collection of works. Very many of the examples already cited are of this kind. In the three searchable fields, (Field One, Title; Field Two, Creator or Composer; Field Three, Performer), information was generally copied from the phonorecording. This is also true of Field Nine, Contents, but in Field Ten, Subject and Tracings, the analysis of the phonorecording is dependent upon the cataloger's lists of appropriate subject headings as well as his need to list all the entries for which additional cards will be made in a unit-card system. In a book catalog, where a main; entry system is used, the index listings will derive from the tracing. In a computerized system, only the subject headings are needed, because the computer can obtain information directly from the entry without requiring additional listing as tracing.

FIELD NINE, CONTENTS

A preliminary decision must be made regarding the extent of analysis needed in this field. A library that does not want to use the system below can modify it as desired. In order to show the full possibilities of analysis, it is necessary to suppose that the library will want each phonorecording completely described so that each band of a phonorecording is included in the catalog as an entry. Even so, the principle of not duplicating information would require that the cataloger understand how the phonorecording has been produced and how the user will look for it.

The first consideration is the amount of uniformity in the phonorecording. A complete work on both sides of a phonodisc by a composer
performed by the artists as listed would not require a contents field at
all. The degree of uniformity is complete. Where two or more works
are included on either side of the phonodisc, the contents field is useful
as a means of making the band containing the second and further works
as accessible as the first. If the composer is the same for all the
works and the performer the same, then the title of each work is not
uniform and the titles must be listed. The principle of uniformity
simply means that no more information is included in the contents
field than is necessary to distinguish the compositions and performers
included. If composer and performer differ as well as title, then all
three would be required in the contents field.

The first decision is whether the phonorecording has a title on the
label or lacking that, on the jacket. If there is a usable title, this
can serve as the unifying feature. The next decision is whether the
work is a single complete work. The possibility of selections must be
considered. Many phonorecordings of lengthy works, such as operas,
masses, oratorios, and ballet suites will include only selections. In
a music research library, it would be very important to identify what
selections are included. This is less important when the user is as
well served by one group of selections as by another. Considerable
caution must be used lest the cataloger find himself required by the
rules of the library to do much research that the user does not need.

The next consideration is whether the phonorecording includes only
one performer or several. A soloist with an orchestra would be considered a single performing group. If there is only one performer, or
group of performers, then the unifying feature is the performer. The
unifying feature may, of course, be the composer. The titles of the
works may vary, along with the performers, but the whole phonorecording may be devoted to the work of one composer.

If the contents field is used, and any complete cataloging would require
it, once a collection of works has been identified, then the decision is
to what extent each band will be separately cataloged. Only selections
must be listed. A complete work, even though it has several parts,
need not be analyzed for Field Nine, Contents. That the work is
complete means that the user will obtain all the selections he wishes,
whatever they may be. Some operas contain very famous passages,
but there is no need in the average library to include these passages
in this field.

A common problem is that the phonorecording has no title whatever, neither on the label nor on the jacket. The first work on each side is taken as the title. Each side is cataloged separately with a note in Field Eight, Additional Description, about the first work on the flip side. This information would not be included in Field Nine, Contents, because everything in this field is searchable, and the result would be a duplication of entries if the note about the flip side were included in Field Nine. The flip side has already been completely cataloged with its own set of entries included in Field Nine.

A phonodisc is divided into Sides and Bands. A phonorecording with one title that includes works on both sides would be cataloged within one entry with complete analysis provided in Field Nine, Contents.

These rules are best shown by examples, beginning with the producer's inclusion of a work to fill out space on a phonodisc devoted to another work.

Example 1

Label title

SIBELIUS   Y1S-36425
Symphony No. 2   ANGEL
The Swan of Tuonela   4
SIR JOHN BARBIROLLI * The Halle Orchestra   Track Tape
Side one (25:27)   3 3/4 IPS
SYMPHONY NO. 2 in D, Op. 43
I.   Allegretto 10:24
II. Tempo Andante, ma rubato 15:03
Side two (28:24)
III. Vivacissimo
20:15
IV. Finale
THE SWAN OF TUONELA
(Lemminkainen Legend, Op. 22 No. 3) 8:09
(English horn solo: Eric Fletcher)

Entry

Symphony in D, no. 2, Op. 43, by Jean Sibelius.
Perf. by John Barbirolli cond. Halle Orchestra.
Angel, Y1S-36425.
7" reel, 4 track, 3 3/4 ips.
Contents: Side 1, Side 2 Band 1, Symphony in D.
Side 2, Band 2, Symphonic work, Lemminkainen
Legend - Selections: "The Swan of Tuonela,"
Op. 22, no. 3.

Note that the word Contents is necessary to identify this field as
searchable. Entries in a manual system would be made as follows:

Symphonic work, Lemminkainen Legend - Selections
"The Swan of Tuonela"
"Lemminkainen Legend"

This differs from the following entry.

Example 2

Septet for piano, trumpet, and strings, Op. 65, by
Camille Saint-Saens. Perf. by The Guilet String
Quartet with Menahem Pressler, Piano, Harry
Glantz, Trumpet, and Philip Sklar, Bass.
Heliodor, H25012.
Side 2 of 12" LPM
With Suite in the Olden Style ... by Vincent D'Indy

In this entry, lacking the word Contents, the information about the
flip side is identified in Field Eight, Additional Description. A
phonodisc may contain a complete work on one side and two other works
on the flip side. The cataloging would indicate this. One entry would
show the flip side in Field Eight, Additional Description, and the other
would show the first work as the entry with the second work included
in Field Nine, Contents.

Example 3

Entry

Symphonic work "In the Steppes of Central Asia," by
Alexander Borodin. Perf. by Kurt Sanderling
cond. Saxon State Orchestra. Heliodor, H25061.
Side 2 of 12" LPM.
With Symphony in B Minor ... by Alexander Borodin.
Contents: Side 2, Band 2: Symphonic work "Romeo and Juliet,"
by Peter Ilyitch Tchaikowsky.

This entry also exemplifies cataloging when the first work serves as
the unit entry. Entries would be made for the second work to provide
access to the uniform title, the conventional title, and the composer.

These examples are not truly collections of works, although they
may be treated very similarly. Collections require a judgment about
the unifying element: title, composer, or performer. Almost all
twelve-inch phonodiscs of popular music are collections of songs by
several different composers with the performer as the unifying element.

Such collections exist for serious music, especially for opera phonorecordings featuring singers.

<u>Example 4</u>

Entry

Operatic arias "Verdi rarities." by Giuseppe Verdi.
Perf. by Monserrat Caballe and Anton Guadagno
cond. RCA Italiana Opera Orchestra and Chorus.
RCA Victor LSC 2995.
12" LPS.
Contents: Side 1, Band 1: Un Giorno di Regno (Il finto
Stanislao) "Ah   non m'hanno ingannato ..." Band 2:
I Lombardi, "Qual prodigio ..." Band 3: I Due Foscari
"No mi Lasciate ..." Band 4: Alzira, "Riposa Tutte, in suo
dolor vegliante ..." Side 2, Band 1: Attila, "Liberamente or
piangi ..." Band 2: Il Corsaro, "Egli no riede ancora ..."
Band 3: Aroldo, "Oh, cielo   Dove son'io "

In this example, the titles of the arias are actually the first words of each of the arias. Entries would be made for each of the arias with the name of the opera preceding, because there is too much likelihood that the first words are the same as the other arias from other operas. There are actually three unifying elements in this phonorecording: the uniform title indicates that all the selections are of the same kind; the composer is the same for all the selections; and there is one performer. The entries for this phonorecording would be as follows:

Verdi, Giuseppe, 1813-1901.
Caballe, Monserrat, Soprano
Guadagno, Anton, cond. RCA Italiana Opera and Chorus
RCA Italiana Opera and Chorus cond. by Anton Guadagno
<u>Un Giorno di Regno</u> (Il Finto Stanislao) "Ah   non m'hanno
   ingannato ..."
<u>Il Finto Stanislao</u> (Un Giorno di Regno)
<u>I Lombardi</u> "Qual prodigio ..."
<u>I Due Foscari</u> "No mi lasciate ..."
<u>Alzira</u> "Riposa Tutte, in suo dolor vegliante ..."
<u>Attila</u> "Liberamente or piangi ..."
<u>Il Corsaro</u> "Egli non riede ancora ..."
<u>Aroldo</u> "Oh, cielo   Dove son'io."

The label provides many more words, in some cases, for each of the arias, but no more is required than necessary to identify the aria. If the name of the opera did not precede the first words of the aria,

more complete listing would be necessary. Although these operas are
very rarely performed and so far have not been recorded, there is no
way that the library can predict what will appear in the future. At one
time the opera <u>Nabucco</u> was never performed in the United States, but
it is now rather popular. The author saw a performance of <u>La</u>
<u>Battaglia de Legnano</u> in Florence, Italy, in 1959. If it was ever re-
corded, interest in the work soon died, despite its many beautiful
passages, but a future audience may demand the opera.

The preceding example is fairly typical of a type of collection,
featuring a famous performer. Collections of operatic arias by many
different composers is more often the rule. Such a phonorecording
would be like the following example.

Example 5

> Waltzes "Waltz " Perf. by Carmen Dragon cond. Hollywood Bowl
> Symphony Orchestra, Capitol Symphony Orchestra. Capitol,
> SP-8623.
> 12" LPS
> Arrangements by Carmen Dragon
> Contents: Side 1, Waltz in E flat, Op. 18, "Grand Valse
> Brilliante," by Chopin. "Valse la Plus Que Lente," by Debussy.
> - Waltz from "Coppelia," by Delibes. - Waltz in A flat, Op. 39
> No. 15, by Brahms. - "Musetta's Waltz Song" from "La
> Boheme," by Puccini. Side 2, Waltz from "Faust," by Gounod.
> - "Valse Triste," by Sibelius. - Waltz in D flat, Op. 64, No. 1,
> "Minute Waltz," by Chopin. - Waltzes from "The Gypsy Baron,"
> by Johann Strauss, Jr.

Entries would be required for each of the composers and each of the
selections as well as entries for Carmen Dragon conducting each of
two orchestras.

A further variation is a collection in which not only are the selections
the work of different composers but the performers differ as well.

In the following example, a further difficulty is that the phonodisc
itself has no title. This must be taken from the jacket.

Example 6

> Operatic arias "Ten Tenors, Ten Arias. "/-Perf. varies-/
> Victor, LM 1202
> 12" LPM
> Jacket title.
> Contents: - Side 1, L'Elisir d'Amore, "Una furtiva lagrima,"

by Donizetti, perf. by Ferruccio Tagliavini, Tenor. - La
Boheme "Che gelida manina," by Puccini, perf. by Mario Lanza,
Tenor. - Carmen "La fleur que tu m'avais jetee," by Bizet,
perf. by James Melton, Tenor. - Tosca " E Lucevan le stelle,"
by Puccini, perf. by Giuseppe di Stefano, Tenor. - Side 2,
Il Trovatore "Di quella pira," by Verdi, perf. by Beniamino
Gigli, Tenor. - Die Meistersinger "Preislied," by Wagner,
perf. by Set Svanholm, Tenor. - Faust "Salut demeure," perf.
by Jussi Bjoerling, Tenor. - Don Giovanni "Il mio tesoro,"
perf. John McCormack, Tenor. - I Pagliacci "Vesti la giubba,"
by Leoncavallo, perf. by Enrico Caruso, Tenor.

Finally, a collection may include compositions of different kinds, the
work of various composers with a variety of performers. The question
that must be decided is whether entries are desired for each of the
compositions, each of the composers, and each of the performers. If
any of these will be omitted as points of access, there is no need to
list them. The following example is completely cataloged, although
there is a question whether such brief selections would justify complete
analysis in Field Nine, Contents.

Example 7

    Collections "Nine classical masterpieces." /-Perf. varies -/
    Phillips 7306 002
    Jacket title.
    Cassette Stereo
    Contents:- Side 1, Operatic choruses Nabucco "Va pensiero
    sull'auri dorate," Chorus of Hebrew slaves, by Verdi; perf. by
    Radio Chorus Leipzig, Herbert Kegel cond. Dresden Philharmonic
    Orchestra. - Song, "Auf Fluegeln des Gesanges," by Mendelssohn;
    perf. by Radio Chorus, Leipzig cond. by Herbert Kegel. -
    Orchestral work "Ball scenes," by Hellmesberger, perf. by
    Robert Hanell cond. Orchestra of the Deutschlandsender. -
    Operatic overture "La gazza ladra" (The thieving magpie), by
    Rossini, perf. by Roberto Benzi cond. Lamoureux Orchestra.
    - Side 2, Suite for Orchestra, Op. 57, "Tsar Saltan," selection
    "Flight of the bumblebee," by Rimsky-Korsakov, perf. by
    Roberto Benzi cond. Monte Carlo Orchestra. - Cavatina Op. 85
    no. 3, by Raff, perf. by Egon Morbitzer, Violin, with Robert
    Hanell cond. Radio Symphony Orchestra, Leipzig. - Suite
    "L'Arlesienne," no. 2 selection "Farandole," by Bizet, Arr. by
    Ernest Guiraud, perf. by Igor Markevitch cond. Lamoureux
    Orchestra. - Operatic overtures "Fra Diavolo," by Auber, perf.
    by Paul Paray cond. Detroit Symphony Orchestra. - Polkas

"Annenpolka," by Johann Strauss, Jr., perf. by Herbert Kegel cond. Dresden Philharmonic Orchestra.

This analysis would require very many entries in the catalog, for each of the uniform titles, for each of the conventional titles, for each of the composers, and for each of the performers. Some of the available information has been omitted here, for instance the name of the librettist, Piave, who wrote <u>Nabucco</u> and the poet, Heinrich Heine, who wrote the words of Mendelssohn's song, "On Wings of Song."

The question whether to include the lyricist as well as the composer is easily resolved. A library policy must establish whether collections of short compositions will be completely analyzed or whether listing by the first composition is desirable. Where the jacket title has been used to identify the phonodisc or casette, a question exists whether the work can be identified best by the first composition.

In the example above, a listing of all the elements was provided: title, composer, and performer. Popular music can generally be cataloged without details of composer and lyricist. The performer is by far more important. Typically the name of the performer serves as the title of the first phonorecording of his performance. Some performers have rather a short life as a recording star, others are much more durable. The example below lists all the songs performed by a singer who seems to have outlasted the crest of his popularity by becoming more respected.

<u>Example 8</u>

Entry

> Popular songs "Pat's Great Hits Vol. 2." Perf. by Pat Boone, vocalist, with orchestra cond. by Billy Vaughn.
> Dot DLP 3261
> 12" LPM
> Contents:- Side 1, A wonderful time up there, - If dreams come true. - For my good fortune. - Cherie, I love you. - When the swallows come back to Capistrano. - Sugar moon. Side 2, It's too soon to know. - April love. - Gee, but it's lonely. - The Mardi Gras march. - I'll remember tonight.

All the information about the composers and the lyricists has been omitted. If they were to be included, adequate reference tools would be necessary so that the first names could be supplied for each where they are lacking.

Label   DOT
PAT'S GREATEST HITS VOL. 2
PAT BOONE

DLP   Side 2
3261   2

1. It's Too Soon To Know
(Deborah Chessler) 2:32
2. April Love
(Webster-Fain) 2:39
3. Gee, But It's Lonely
(Phil Everly) 2:17
4. That's How Much I Love You
(Arnold-Fowler-Hall) 1:54
5. The Mardi Gras March
(Webster-Fain) 2:04
6. I'll Remember Tonight
(Webster-Fain) 2:20

The flip side is similar in providing the names of the composer and the lyricist, if they are different. Except for Phil Everly and Deborah Chessler, no first names are given. The title of this phonorecording identifies the performer, so that in brief-form cataloging this would be the first element:

Boone, Pat: "Pat's greatest hits, vol. 2." Billy Vaughn and orchestra. Dot DLP 3261. 12" LPM. Includes Side 1, "A wonderful time up there." and Side 2, "April love."

In this abbreviated form of cataloging, the uniform titles can serve equally as subject headings to categorize the kinds of phonorecordings. The contents are listed as desired by the library.

In the example below, the name of the performer is the title of the phonorecording.

Example 9   DECCA STEREO

Label: W. C. FIELDS

THE ORIGINAL VOICE TRACKS
FROM HIS GREATEST MOVIES

DL 79164   Side 1
7-11682   1. The Philosophy of W. C. Fields
2. The "Sound" of W. C. Fields
3. The Rascality of W. C. Fields
4. The Chicanery of W. C. Fields

The brief-form cataloging of this phonodisc would put the name of
the performer first and omit the listing of the contents of each side.
This would be very much like the full-scale cataloging of the phonorecording, because the contents of each side do not constitute a separate
and readily identified work. The contents explain how the phonorecording was put together. There is no means, short of lengthy research,
of identifying the sound tracks from which the phonorecording was
made.

Entry:

> Monologues "W. C. Fields, the original voice tracks from his
> greatest movies." Perf. by W. C. Fields.
> Decca DL 79164
> 12" LPS.

An entry would be made for Fields, W. C., Comedian.

The following example presents another problem.

Example 10

Label: The original sound track
                               CHARLES CHAPLIN'S
                           A COUNTESS FROM HONG KONG
                              A Universal Release

                          Music Arranged and Conducted by
                                Lambert Williamson
DECCA   DL 1501 Side 2
          1. Change Partners (3:46-AS)
          2. Bonjour Madame (2:18-AS)
          3. (a) Hudson Goes to Bed
              (b) The Ill Fitting Dress (2:40-AS)
          4. The Countess Sleeps (2:00-AS)
          5. Gypsy Caprice (3:50-AS)
          6. A Countess From Hong Kong (1:58-AS)
          7. (a) My Star (b) Tango Natasha (4:18-AS)
                          Produced for Records
                             by Milt Gabler

The featured name is not that of a performer but of the composer.
Although Charles Chaplin carved an enduring niche for himself in the
history of the motion picture, he would be noted in the cataloging of
this phonodisc as the composer. He was the director, rather than
star, of the motion picture from the sound track of which this phonorecording was made.

Entry:

> Sound Track "A Countess from Hong Kong," by Charles Chaplin.
> Perf. by Lambert Williamson, Cond.
> Decca DL 1501.
> Original Universal release.

No contents note was made for this phonodisc, because it can be assumed that all of the score was included, except for the repetition of the various parts. A listing of the contents would not greatly aid the user, who can inspect the phonodisc if he wishes to learn what the names of the different sections of the score are.

However in the following example, a contents note is made listing all the different songs. Note that the label includes the name of the composer, who is also the performer, after each of the song titles.

Example 11

> Comic songs "That Was the Year That Was," by Tom Lehrer.
> Perf. by Tom Lehrer. Reprise

Label:

REPRISE RECORDS
THAT WAS THE YEAR THAT WAS
TOM LEHRER

RS 6179   Side
                                                                      1

> 1. National Brotherhood Week (Tom Lehrer)
> 2. MLF Lullaby (Tom Lehrer)
> 3. George Murphy (Tom Lehrer)
> 4. The Folk Song Army (Tom Lehrer)
> 5. Smut (Tom Lehrer)
> 6. Send the Marines (Tom Lehrer)
> 7. Pollution (Tom Lehrer)

STEREO

Entry:

> Comic Songs "That Was the Year That Was," by Tom Lehrer.
> Perf. by Tom Lehrer vocalist. Reprise RS 6179.
> 12" LPS
> Contents: Side 1, National Brotherhood Week. - MLF
> Lullaby. - George Murphy. - The Folk Song Army. - Smut. -
> Send the Marines. - Pollution. - Side 2, ...

A computer would retrieve Tom Lehrer either as performer or as composer. In a manual system, it would be necessary to list Tom Lehrer only once, although the example as shown, or "Perf. by the composer," is necessary to inform the user of the catalog that the composer sings and accompanies himself in the performance of the songs he has written. This would be shown in Field Ten, Tracings.

FIELD TEN, POINTS OF ACCESS OR TRACINGS

In a manual system, to account for all the different entries filed in the card catalog, a listing of these must be made. In the unit-card system explained throughout this book, all the entries are of equal value. There are no main entries and there are no entries added to the main entry, because each is considered a point of access, along with the subject analysis provided.

Many libraries would find the system of uniform titles recommended to be rather far from the present style of cataloging. These uniform titles are useful in that many works have no conventional title and the title of a phonodisc is commonly the title of the work performed. Such uniform titles may be used as subject headings, along with those suggested below.

Uniform titles always show the form of composition or the type of phonorecording. Spoken records, phonorecordings of animal or other sounds, and the great variety of phonorecordings of popular music can be arranged in a book catalog without using a uniform title for each entry. Each section can be so designated and the other entries can show only the title of the phonorecording. A card catalog presents another problem, so that the decision not to employ uniform titles would mean that the list of subject headings is greatly lengthened.

In the examples used, the kinds of entries were included to show the number of points of access required in complete cataloging for users who will need phonorecordings not only for the composition but also for the performers. A typing problem arises with the proliferation of entries, the tracings at times requiring as much space as the entry itself. It is wise to use the back of the card, with the hole at the top, as the space for typing tracings, especially if some choice is made between those names shown in the unit entry and the ones listed as points of access.

Because a performer is listed with the instrument he uses or his voice range, the entry serves as a kind of guide to the medium of performance.   The best way to show the medium of performance is with a list of subject headings.   Both the uniform titles and the subject headings provide a key to the contents of a phonorecording, the uniform title being restricted to the form of composition and the subject to the instrument or the medium of performance.

A suggested list of uniform titles and of subject headings is given in this chapter with an explanation of the various kinds of uniform titles, those used especially with collections of works on one side of a phono-recording and those used for single works, often serving as the only title a phonorecording has.   The list of subject headings is also explained.

Uniform Titles

Used only for the form of composition or the kind of phonorecording. As suggested for phonorecording of music, the singular would indicate one composition only, the plural would indicate several.   If the uni-form title is used as a subject heading, or the title of a section of a book catalog, the plural would be preferable.   The plural is shown if it requires more change than the addition of an (s).

Adagio(s) - A slow movement in a symphony, also a composition so
    named, a portion of a ballet;   for other tempo markings see
    Symphony, below.
Allemandes (singular or plural) - A kind of dance, usually quite short,
    similar to a gigue or bourree;   no longer popular.
Aria(s) - A show vocal piece for solo singer, often derived from an
    opera or an oratorio.
Ballade(s) - A composition derived from the French word for ballad.
    May be used for solo instruments.   If a vocal work, the word "Song"
    is preferable.
Ballet - Music especially written for the performance of dances, often
    in story form.
Ballet Suite - Either may be used, the former for a complete ballet,
    the latter for a selection of passages from a ballet.
Capriccio - Usually a spirited work for solo instrument, frequently
    the violin.
Chorus, Chorale - A work for several voices.   Chorus is also a
    subject heading, because the word may refer the group as well as
    to the type of composition.   Chorales are usually found in oratorios
    or as separate composition.

Composition(s) - Used for collections of several different kinds of
    music. This is vague and should not be used when the works have
    something more in common than indicated by this word.
Concertino(s) - A small concerto. The word is the diminutive form
    of "concerto." It may be quite short.
Concerto, Concerto da chiesa, Concerto grosso (plural Concerti) - A
    composition for orchestra and one or possibly two or three solo
    instruments is called a concerto. A concerto da chiesa is rarely
    found in recorded music: literally, a concerto of the church.
    Concerti grossi is used for music usually from the Baroque or
    preclassical period, many of them by George Friedrich Handel.
Dance, Dances, Dance Music - Used for popular music or serious
    music where different kinds of dances are included. If only one
    kind, for instance, Waltz or Cha-cha or Samba, use that name
    if desired. For a very small collection, the word dance may be
    sufficient.
Divertimento (plural, Divertimenti) - A short composition not follow-
    ing the standard form for other compositions; many were written
    by Mozart.
Duet, Duo(s) - A duet indicates that a pair of the same instruments
    are used, a duo indicates that there are two different instruments.
    Two voices are always a duet, and the expression Duo pianos is
    common, although rather confusing; Duet for piano would be more
    explicit.
Excerpt(s) - Used to show a condensed version of a longer work, as
    Opera-excerpts.
Fantasy (plural, Fantasies) - May be given in French or Italian as
    Fantaisie or Fantasia. Do not use the old spelling, phantasy,
    which has come to mean a literary work. This is a composition
    of relatively free form.
Impromptu(s) - Compositions by Chopin have this title, indicating a
    short work of relatively free form.
Improvisation(s) - Originally this was a composition prepared on the
    spur of the moment by a performer. Such works should include
    the date because quite often they cannot be exactly repeated. Jazz
    is a kind of group inprovisation.
Incidental Music - The music that was written for various plays, such
    as either of Grieg's Peer Gynt Suites or Mendelssohn's Midsummer
    Night's Dream.
Intermezzo (plural, Intermezzi) - Literally, in the middle, a work
    that is played in the middle of another work, such as the
    "Intermezzo" from Cavalleria Rusticana.
Invention - A term used by Bach and other composers for a brief work
    usually for solo instrument.

Lieder, Canciones, Chansons, Canzoni - The word for "songs" in
German, Spanish, French, and Italian, respectively. The use of
these terms would distinguish not only the language, but to some
extent the style. The word 'Songs' can be used for all four,
although it is customary to separate Lieder from other kinds of
songs.

Madrigal(s) - A kind of song, usually sung by a group, written during
the late Renaissance. Madrigals are highly specialized songs and
generally distinguished from other kinds.

Magnificat(s) - The musical setting of a specific passage from the
Gospel of St. Luke, usually in Latin. It may be sung by a soloist
and chorus. The word is a Latin verb, but it has been anglicized
and may be given in the plural form of English nouns.

March (plural, Marches) - A composition in 4/4 time, often played by
a band.

Mass (plural, Masses) - The musical setting of the rites of the
Catholic Church. Like an oratorio, a mass is usually performed
by soloists, chorus, and orchestra.

Mazurka, Polonaise(s) - Polish dances used as the basis for compositions for solo instrument, especially the piano.

Melody (plural, Melodies) - Used for the title of compositions as well
as one of the necessary components of music, for instance "Melody
in F," by Anton Rubinstein.

Military Music - This is a generic term for horn calls, ruffles and
flourishes, fanfares, marches, and other music used in military
ceremonies.

Musical Comedy - A kind of American operetta as currently produced,
distinguished from the operettas of Victor Herbert, for instance.

Minuet(s) - A movement of a symphony, sometimes given in the
Italian ("menuetto") or separate composition. A minuet was a slow,
graceful dance, popular in the eighteenth century, although modern
composers such as Paderewski have written minuets.

Nocturne(s) - From a French word for a composition to be played at
night.

Opera, Grand Opera, Opera Buffa, Comic Opera(s) - A drama set to
music. Prefer the term "Opera" to "Grand Opera," and "Comic
Opera" to "Opera Buffa." The word is derived from Latin, the
plural of a noun meaning a work. In Italian, as well as Latin, the
complete works of an author are given the title "Opera." Operas
are performed by soloists, chorus, and orchestra. The term
"Chamber Opera" indicates a small group.

Operetta(s) - A work that includes spoken passages as well as music.
This term may be reserved for German works, the works of Victor

Herbert in this form, and the works of Arthur Sullivan in collaboration with William Schwenk Gilbert.

Oratorio(s) - A lengthy work on a sacred theme for soloists, chorus, and orchestra, for instance, The Messiah, by George Friedrich Handel.

Overture(s), Prelude(s) - A composition that introduces an opera, operetta, musical comedy, or oratorio. An overture concludes before the curtain rises, and a prelude continues into the music of the first scene. Each may be written as a separate composition, for instance, "Prelude in C sharp minor," by Sergei Rachmaninoff.

Partita(s) - A work for solo instrument, usually short in length, often extremely difficult to perform. The word is from the Latin, meaning divided into parts.

Polka(s) - A dance in 3/4 time, very rapid and energetic. Polkas are one kind of popular music, along with other dance forms.

Quartet(s) - A work for four instruments or voices.

Quintet(s) - A work for five instruments or voices.

Requiem(s), Requiem Mass (plural Requiem Masses) - A composition in honor of the dead, a kind of funeral music. A requiem may follow any form, but a Requiem Mass follows the form of the Catholic church service.

Rhapsody (plural Rhapsodies) - A work that does not follow a prescribed form for solo instrument or for orchestra.

Romance - A short composition for solo instrument; like Melody.

Rondo (plural, Rondi) - A portion of a symphony or a concerto, also written as a separate work. A rondo has a prescribed form of theme and variations.

Sacred Music - The generic term for Hymns, Requiems, Sacred Cantatas, and other music played in churches.

Scherzo (plural, Scherzi) - From the Italian word for joke. A movement of a symphony following a prescribed form or a separate composition, usually brisk.

Selection(s) - Used for a portion of a longer work. Do not use for a collection of works in the same form or for one instrument.

Septet(s) - A work for seven instruments.

Serenade(s) - A work to be performed in the evening, from the Latin word for evening. The opposite was Aubade, to be played at dawn. Serenades and Aubades were supposed to be performed in the open for the entertainment of another person, although Aubade is quite rare now.

Sextet(s) - A work for six instruments or voices.

Sinfonia(s) - From the Italian for symphony, used at times to distinguish a work that is relatively free form from a work that follows the classic form of the symphony.

Sinfonietta(s) - A little symphony, used for brief works in symphonic
    form.
Sonata(s) - A composition for solo instrument, sometimes with accom-
    paniment. The sonata form was relatively fixed by Beethoven's
    time, but has been greatly varied since then.
Sonatina(s) - A little sonata, a shorter version of the sonata form.
Song(s) - A work for voice with accompaniment, not extracted from a
    longer work. May be modified as Popular Songs, Comic Songs,
    Folk Songs, Country (Western) Songs, etc.
Suite(s) - A group of selections from a longer work, or a work,
    usually for orchestra, divided into several parts.
Symphonic poem, Tone poem(s) - Also called "program music,"
    because the work follows a literary plan or is explicative of some
    facet of life. Such works almost always have a conventional title,
    usually given by the composer.
Symphony (plural, Symphonies) - A work for orchestra divided into
    movements which may be labeled according to the tempo, as
    Allegro, Adagio, Andante, Larghetto, Largo. A movement played
    as a single work may bear the title Andante, for instance, from
    Mahler's Symphony No. 5. This should be listed as a selection,
    Symphonies-Selections, if a part of the contents of a single phono-
    disc. The tempo may be used to identify selections from other
    works.
Toccata, Fugue(s) - A fugue, from the Latin word for flight, may be
    written for almost any instrument or group of instruments, but it
    is especially important, as is Toccata, for organ music. Both
    forms are fully prescribed, as are such other forms as
    Passacaglia, and may be used in orchestral or other works.
Trio, Trio Sonata, Triple Sonata(s) - Used for three instruments or
    voices. A trio sonata differs from a sonata in which three instru-
    ments play. A trio for strings is different in form from a trio
    sonata.
Variations - Sometimes the word "Theme" precedes Variations. The
    singular is not used. Where "Theme and variations" is given as
    the conventional title of a work, it is better to use the word
    Variations as a uniform title.
Waltz - A dance in 3/4 time (as is the Tango), often played by full
    symphony orchestra.

Whether used as the category heading in a book catalog or for the
unit entry of cards in a card catalog, the uniform title should be taken
from the label of the phonodisc wherever possible. The plural form
would indicate a collection of one form. Where many different kinds
of forms are included in a collection the word Compositions can be

used. Such terms as Medley, Potpourri, and Anthology are rather
misleading and should be reserved for label titles, where they are most
often used.

In the examples used throughout the text, full cataloging of which is
provided in Chapter 9, a variety of uniform titles have been shown,
such as "Comic Songs" used for the works of Tom Lehrer. In general
the cataloger must avoid using uniform titles that would represent a
judgment of the value of the work. This same uniform title used for a
phonorecording of arias sung by Florence Foster Jenkins would constitute a kind of editorial comment by the cataloger. Other uniform titles
for spoken records and for sound effects are: Addresses, Lectures,
Orations, and the more general Speeches. The word Speeches may be
used when the precise form is not known. Orations have gone out of
style and would rarely be found as a label title.

Poetry - Use for readings of poetry whether by the author or by
    another person.
Prose - Use for readings of prose selections.
Readings - Use for a mixture of prose and poetry included as the
    contents of a phonorecording.
Drama, Comedy, Tragedy - Use for dramatic works, rather than the
    vague and ambiguous word "Plays." The word Drama would be
    preferable if there is a relatively small collection of works. If
    desired, the form of the drama may be specified as Comedy or
    Tragedy. A collection of these works, if any exist, would require
    the plural, Comedies and Tragedies. Dramas is acceptable
    English.
Monologue(s) - Use for a single speaker, especially the phonorecord-
    ings of comic routines.
Debate(s) - Use only for the formal kind of argument. Dialogue,
    Hearings, Trial, may be used for informal argument and testimony.
Animal Sounds, Bird Song, Sound Effects - Use these uniform titles
    for phonorecordings that are respectively devoted to the cries of
    animals, the songs of birds, or a mixture of sounds.

As indicated above, the uniform titles suggested here may be used as
subject headings where the title of the work does not duplicate the
uniform title. There are arguments against such a proceeding in a
unit-card system, the chief of which is that subject headings by medium
of performance align perfectly with uniform titles that specify the form
of composition. If the two are kept separate, the complementary
function of the subject heading with the uniform title is lost in the
alphabetic arrangement of the card catalog.

Subject Headings

In the kind of cataloging described here, especially suited to a computerized system, Field Ten, Access, would contain only subject headings. For several uniform titles, no subject heading is required. Such uniform titles as "Opera, Operetta, Musical Comedy, Cantata, and Mass, Requiem Mass, Oratorio" are for soloists, chorus, and orchestra. They can be so defined, so that a subject heading is added only if there is some variation from this; for instance, Berlioz wrote a requiem for male voices only. This would mean that a subject heading should be added for a phonorecording of this work. Similarly, a symphony is written for an orchestra of a special kind. A subject heading would be superfluous, except for the unusual symphonies that include soloists or choruses, or both.

The list of subject headings explained below can be divided into four groups that specify the medium of performance: headings for voices, headings for kinds of orchestras, and headings for instruments of solo performers, and a general category for headings used with sound effect phonorecordings, recordings of animal sounds, and spoken records. A fifth kind of subject heading will also be discussed: headings that do not describe the medium of performance but generalize about the kind of music or the kind of spoken record, such as "French drama," "Italian language instruction," "Humor in music," and "Instructional works."

As noted above, all of the first three of the four groups of subject headings specify what the performers use to make the sounds reproduced on the phonorecording, whether voices, instruments, or other things. Subject headings may be combined and listed together in alphabetical order except for the instrument (or instruments) used as accompaniment. For instance, a concerto for violin, cello, and piano, such as Beethoven's "Triple Concerto" would have the subject heading "Cello, Piano, Violin & Orchestra." The ampersand (&) is used because it is disregarded in filing, and the Orchestra is regarded as the accompaniment, hence placed last, after the ampersand. For Beethoven's Symphony no. 9, the subject heading would be "Baritone, Contralto, Soprano, Tenor Voices, Mixed Chorus & Orchestra."

1. Voices

Distinction is made between male voices and female voices, with a combination described as "mixed." The word voice must be added when the subject heading is used alone for the voice range:

    Soprano voice
    Mezzo-soprano voice
    Contralto voice
    Counter-tenor voice
    Tenor voice
    Baritone voice
    Bass voice

   Note that such terms as "Lyric" or "Coloratura" are not used here,
although that possibility exists for libraries with very large collections
of phonorecordings for voices. The word "Alto" has not been used here,
to reduce the ambiguity that exists in these words for voices. There is
a Baritone Horn, a Bass Viol, a Bass Drum, and a Tenor and a Soprano
Saxophone. Alto is used for Alto Horn.

   Combinations of voices include duets with the orchestra or instru-
ment(s) accompanying the voices included after the ampersand:

    Baritone, Tenor Voices & ...
    Baritone, Bass Voices & ...
    Contralto, Soprano Voices & ...
    Contralto, Tenor Voices & ...
    Soprano, Baritone Voices & ...
    Soprano, Tenor Voices & ...

In this arrangement the female voice is listed before the male voice,
two male or two female voices are given in alphabetical order. A
duet for bass voice and contralto would be listed as "Bass, Contralto
Voices & ...," with the accompaniment following. Many libraries
prefer to list the voices in order of voice range, but in a card catalog
this would separate cards for the phonorecordings of voices rather than
keeping them together. Trios would include a wide range of possibilities, but a quartet would be limited to one or at most two possibilities.
Since this is the case, the subject heading "Voice quartet" can be used,
so that rather than provide the subject heading "Baritone, Contralto,
Soprano, Tenor," for Beethoven's Ninth Symphony, it is sufficient to
list Voice Quartet, Mixed Chorus, & Orchestra.

   The word "Chorus" may be used for the form of the work as well as
the medium of performance. There is no confusion, generally, except
when the uniform title "Chorus" is used. For this uniform title, the
subject heading Mixed Voices, or Male Voices, or Female Voices,
respectively, can be used. The same is true of Chorales, trios of
voices, quartets, quintets, sextets, and even octets. A famous
passage for eight female voices occurs in the opera, Die Walkuere
(The Valkyrie) by Richard Wagner. If a phonorecording of that

passage were obtained, the uniform title would be "Operatic octets," and the subject heading would be "Female voices."

The list of subject headings includes "Boys' Choirs," as well as "Children's Voices," for phonorecordings that would require them. As noted elsewhere in this book, where the voice range is a problem, especially for popular music, the correct subject heading would be Vocalist, either Female or Male as needed. The subject heading for a group would be either Male Vocal Group, Female Vocal Group, or Mixed Vocal Group, whichever most accurately describes the medium of performance. Musical Groups can be used to identify performers of popular groups who sing and accompany themselves. This term may also be used with the name of the group when it would clarify what might be a puzzling name: Jefferson Airplane (Musical Group).

2. Instruments

The instruments of a symphony orchestra are separated into four groups: "String Instruments," "Woodwind Instruments," "Brass Instruments," and "Percussion Instruments." The string instruments are either scraped with a bow or, in the case of the harp, plucked. Modern composers may include almost any instrument in the score, and sometimes sounds are produced from almost anything from crashing china to a musical saw, played with a bow like a string instrument.

The common string instruments are:

Violin
Viola
Cello
Bass Viol
Harp

These are the subject headings employed, rather than such possibilities as Violoncello (the correct term), where Cello, the abbreviation, has become so fixed in the English language that very few people refer to the instrument by its full name, preferring a word that is, in fact, a diminutive ending common in Italian. Bass Viol is preferred to Double Bass; Bull Fiddle, while humorous, is worse, and Fiddle should be avoided in any case.

There are many woodwind instruments, but at least some of these would be included in performance of a symphony:

Flute
Clarinet
Oboe
English Horn
Bassoon
Contra-Bassoon
Saxophone
Piccolo

The saxophone is infrequently used in a symphony orchestra. A composition for solo, or even accompanied, piccolo would probably be difficult for the average person to listen to. These subject headings are included here because they may be necessary, and this list is not available elsewhere.

The brass instruments are:

Trumpet
Cornet
Bugle
French Horn
Alto Horn
Trombone
Baritone Horn
Tuba

There are other brass instruments, but these are used regularly, and solo works exist for most of them.

There are many percussion instruments, some as well known as the Piano, some that are used only rarely, and a few that might best be described by the subject heading "Chance Instruments." They are listed here, although a solo work for any of these, excepting the most common, would be quite unusual, marking the composer as a kind of adventurer in music:

Bass drum
Bells
Bongo Drum
Castanets
Chimes
Cymbals
Marimba
Snare Drum
Steel Drum
Triangle

Tympani
Xylophone

The Library of Congress list of subject headings includes many that are quite rare. Some of the common ones not listed above are:

Piano
Harpsichord
Organ
Accordion
Bagpipe
Guitar
Mandolin

Others are rather rare because of their age, such as

Lute
Viola da Gamba
Clavichord

And many are foreign, such as

Sitar
Samisen
Koto
Pi-pa
Ch'in

all of Oriental origin, and

Balalaika

the Russian stringed instrument, and the

Zither

a kind of middle European harp.

There are several electronic instruments, demonstrating the same sort of inventiveness that produced the

Glass Harmonica

and the

Pyrophone

One of the first was the "Ondes Martenot" (Martenot waves), named for the man who invented it. A popular instrument at present is the "Moog Synthesizer." These instruments may be grouped together as:

Electronic Instruments.

Instrumental groups are indicated by the following subject headings.

Orchestra	Use for a combination of instruments including stringed instruments as well as brass, woodwind, and percussion instruments.
Band	Use for a combination of instruments excluding stringed instruments.
Dance Orchestra	Use for a combination of instruments assembled to perform popular music.
Dance Band	Use for a group excluding stringed instruments assembled to perform popular music.
Brass Band	Brass Band indicates that the composition of the group includes other instruments but the brass instruments predominate.
Chamber Orchestra	Use for a small group of instruments including string and other instruments. Prefer this to Little Orchestra or Little Symphony Orchestra.
Instrumental Group	Use for several different instruments (more than eight). This heading is useful for a collection of several different kinds of groups featured in phonorecordings.
Brass Instruments Percussion Instruments String Instruments Woodwind Instruments	Use for phonorecordings of music played by one kind of instrument, regardless of the make-up of the group. If brass instruments and other instruments, such as percussion are included, prefer Brass band.
String Orchestra	Use for a combination of strings and other instruments, such as percussion and piano.

String Quartet   Use for four stringed instruments.

Steel band   Use for a group of tuned steel drums
                            played as percussion instruments.

For a group of instruments of the same kind, such as Violins, the
word Ensemble can be used.

Violin Ensemble
Woodwind Ensemble
Brass Ensemble

As indicated above, a group of instruments such as musical saws,
kazoos, washboards, and jugs can be called "Chance Instruments" or
"Chance Instrumental Ensemble."

3. Other Subject Headings

Spoken records require special subject headings. Phonorecordings
used for language instruction should be given subject headings following this pattern:

(LANGUAGE) Language Instruction

such as French Language Instruction, Italian Language Instruction,
German Language Instruction. The same pattern can be used for
French poetry, comedies, drama, and prose. French Language would
be the general subject heading so that the uniform title would separate
the different forms of literature. Other spoken record subject headings are of less significance. If a uniform title is used, it will make
further analysis unnecessary for several different kinds of phonorecordings. English Language would be appropriate as a subject heading for
the catalog of a library that contained phonorecordings of works in
several different languages. It would not be necessary if the library
included only English language works in its collection of spoken records.

Other subject headings may include such things as:

Train Whistles
Wolves

and the names of other animals.

The uniform title will often be sufficient (for instance, Sound Effects)
when a subject entry is needed for a phonorecording, while the general
rule holds that uniform titles indicate the form of the works included
on a phonorecording, reserving subject headings for the medium of
performance. Because Field Nine, Contents, precedes Field Ten,

Access (or Tracing), there is no need to include even the words
Composer and Title Analytics. The fact that the phonorecording has
been analyzed to account for all the works included is sufficient indication that an entry will be found for each name and title listed.

SUMMARY

   Fields Nine and Ten are the last two searchable fields, complemen-
ting the information found in Field One, Title: Field Two, Composer;
and Field Three, Performer. With an understanding of these five
fields, plus the usefulness of the features of identification in Field
Four, Producer-Distributor; Field Five, Label number; Field Six,
Physical Description; and Field Eight, Additional Description, the
student is prepared to undertake the cataloging of phonorecordings.
The system used here, as explained in the Introduction, is recommended
as a usable system that will provide maximum access to the contents
of phonorecordings, but it is not offered as a standardized system.
That does not exist, so far, even though there is great effort to en-
courage the adoption of the Library of Congress system. Many catalogers have found the cataloging of the Library of Congress to be
either too elaborate or too sketchy for their purposes. The cataloger
who understands the nature of phonorecordings can readily adapt himself to any method of cataloging, and generally improve it, while the
student trained to follow one prescribed method as a series of hard
and fast rules will find that he is out of his depth everywhere except in
a library that follows the same rules.

Chapter 8

LIBRARY OF CONGRESS CATALOGING

Since 1958 when the Library of Congress first included its cataloging of phonorecordings as a section of the National Union Catalogue, some help has been available for those libraries that find the cards prepared by the Library of Congress satisfactory for their purposes. The decision whether to use the preprinted cards depends on the extent to which the purchase of cards is justified by the circumstances in a given library.

These points must be carefully considered:

a. Will the collection consist almost entirely of phonorecordings purchased from commercial sources in the United States? A library with an extensive collection of locally prepared phonorecordings will find that the trouble of ordering cards cannot be justified by the amount of help they provide.

b. Does the library already use Library of Congress subject headings? A library that uses the Sears list or an extensive revision of the Library of Congress list will incur problems by employing Library of Congress cards that must be heavily revised before they are usable. It is easier to do original cataloging than to revise cataloging already completed that is quite different from what the library needs.

c. Will emphasis be placed on access to the collection by means of performer? The Library of Congress bases its cataloging on rules developed at the turn of the century for music in printed form. The Anglo-American Cataloging Rules of 1967 include the latest revisions of these rules, but little attention is given the performer. Library of Congress cataloging is a main entry system with entries either under the composer or the title of the phonorecording. This method of cataloging is quite similar to brief listing in many respects, especially in treating phonorecordings that are not serious music. A library that wishes to provide users with access to the collection not only by composers but also by performers would find the Library of Congress cards insufficient or unreliable.

d. Will a number of cards be used for cataloging phonorecordings to provide access by compositions included in a collection? Included in this consideration is the number of cards that will be needed for listing performers. Library of Congress cards are not cheap, and even if the library gets one card and prepares many copies by xerox, or another method, the cost can run very high. The library would find its costs reduced by duplicating cards with a small mimeographed machine whenever several cards, more than six or seven, are needed.

e. Will users understand Library of Congress cards? Closely similar is the question whether the cataloger can follow the methods used by the Library of Congress. Cards must be prepared locally when not available from the Library of Congress. This includes not only cards for locally prepared phonorecordings that must be cataloged but also phonorecordings from foreign sources. In order to prepare cards consistently, the library must follow the Library of Congress procedures faithfully, using the Anglo-American Cataloging Rules of 1967. There is a risk that neither the user nor the cataloger will be able to understand these rules well enough to apply them consistently. Experienced catalogers often take issue with the Library of Congress, and each other, on the interpretation of the rules.

f. Will delays in the ordering and receipt of cards work no hardship on the user and the library? Cataloging must always be done promptly in libraries that are continually acquiring new materials, lest unwanted duplicates be purchased because the records are insufficient. It is not possible to make accurate predictions about the Library of Congress and the speed with which orders for cards are filled. Many things have happened in the past to delay orders, and it is safe to say that they may happen again, from delays at the U.S. Copyright Office to changes of processing routines within the Library of Congress.

If the library can give positive answers to these questions and if Library of Congress cards are generally used for books or for motion pictures, then using the Library of Congress preprinted cards may result in a saving of time and possibly of money. The collection should be relatively small, limited to phonorecordings purchased from commercial sources and manufactured in the United States; the library should already be using Library of Congress cards and the subject headings found on them; and there should be no need to rush to catalog the phonorecordings. It will be necessary first to find

Library of Congress card order numbers, a searching task that may present many difficulties. In order to use the National Union Catalog listing of phonorecordings, a thorough familiarity with the Anglo-American Cataloging Rules of 1967 is advisable. The summary below will not substitute for study of the rules.

The main entry is derived from the rules for books and for music in printed form. A composition with a single composer is regarded as similar to a book with the composer considered to be a kind of author. Compositions that embody the work of a poet, dramatist, scenarist, such as musical comedies, operas, ballets, and songs are entered under the composer. An added entry is made for the name of the poet or dramatist who provided the words for the composition.

A work with two or more composers is entered according to the rule for the entry of books of multiple authorship. That is, the more important composer is chosen as the main entry and other composers, but no more than two, are listed as added entries. If another composer has transcribed or orchestrated the work of a given composer, the entry will be under the name of the original composer with the transcriber, orchestrator, arranger, or whatever appearing as an added entry. Anonymously composed works are entered under title, except for arrangements of folk music, which are entered under the name of the composer who provided the arrangement.

A further exception is made when the transcription is virtually a different work, such as variations based on the theme of another composer or even the cadenzas provided by a performer for a concerto. Such works would be entered not under the original composer but under the name of the composer who is responsible for the later work. However, an added entry is provided for the original composer with the name of the composer of the later work serving as main entry.

Music used in the rituals of various churches is entered under the name of the church, for instance "Catholic Church" with the words "liturgy and ritual" added to the heading. Collections are generally entered under the title of the collection, that is the title of the phonorecording. By providing added entries, after a main entry has been selected, the cataloger is able to maximize the access to the collection in a given library. However, the National Union Catalog is arranged only by main entries, so that a searcher must be prepared to try various approaches when trying to find the cataloging for a problematic item.

The most noticeable difference between the catalog cards for books and those for music, whether phonorecordings or printed scores, is

the provision of space for a uniform title or for the adopted form of a
conventional title. The Library of Congress prints its cards so that
the uniform title is enclosed in brackets and space is left for libraries
to include another or different uniform title if that is desirable. Uniform titles that include a prescribed form of conventional titles provide
a means of listing works together despite differences of language and
usage that may be found in phonorecordings. A list of uniform titles
is determined by the preferred entry for each composition, usually
the first title used in the catalog with the form of composition preferred
to a conventional title. That is, Beethoven's "Moonlight Sonata" would
be listed as "Sonata, piano, no. 14, op. 27, no. 2, C sharp minor."
The Library of Congress would include the musical sign that indicates
a sharp.

A part of the uniform title is the medium of performance, as exemplified above. Provisions are made for variety of instruments, such as
string trios. The title as found on the item is given in the lines following the space left for the uniform title. Performers are not included
except as notes, but the phonorecording company is shown along with the
number of the item, usually the producer's series number. The
Library of Congress always includes a word such as phonodisc, phonotape, phonowire, or phonoroll in italics after the title of the item, if
there is no uniform title, or after the uniform title if there is one. A
further provision is that the date of the phonorecording be included
following the producer's series number. A date may be approximated
if not readily available.

In the remainder of this chapter, complete Library of Congress
cataloging is provided for many of the examples included in previous
chapters. Study of these examples and comparisons with the cataloging
as explained in the text should enable the reader to understand the
methods of the Library of Congress sufficiently. Note the large number
of notes that include performers and other details and the lack of
uniform titles for collections of all kinds and for phonorecordings that
are not primarily serious music. Special attention should be paid to
the subject headings listed and their importance in the Library of
Congress cataloging of phonorecordings. Compositions that are the
same are included even though the rest of the information is different.

Mozart, Johann Chrysostom Wolfgang Amadeus, 1756-1799
[Symphony, K. 551. C major] Phonodisc.
Symphony no. 41, in C major (Jupiter)
Symphony no. 35, in D major, K. 385
(Haffner) Columbia ML 5655 [1961]
2s. 12 in. 33 1/3 rpm microgroove (Columbia masterworks)
Columbia Symphony Orchestra; Bruno Walter, Conductor
Duration: 30 min. 15 sec. and 18 min. 55 sec. respectively
Program notes by David Johnson on Slipcase.
I. Symphonies - To 1800. I. Mozart, Johann Chrysostom
Wolfgang Amadeus. Symphony K. 385. D Major. II. Columbia
Symphony Orchestra. III. Walter, Bruno, 1876-

Uniform title is shown in brackets. Note its difference from label
title as shown on following line.

Sibelius, Jean, 1865-1957
[Symphony, no. 5, op. 82, E flat major] Phonodisc.
Symphony no. 5, in E Flat major, op. 82.
Finlandia, Symphonic poem, op. 26. Angel Records 35922.
[1961]
2s. 12 in. 33 1/3 rpm microgroove. Stereophonic
Philharmonia Orchestra; Herbert von Karajan, conductor
Recorded in England
Program notes by Andrew Porter on slipcase.
1. Symphonies. 2. Symphonic poems.
I. Sibelius, Jean. 1865-1957. Finlandia. II. Philharmonia
Orchestra. London. III. Karajan, Herbert von. IV. Title:
Finlandia.

Note difference of order of elements in uniform title and label title.
Also note compositions included.

Berlioz, Hector, 1803-1869
[Harold en Italie] Phonodisc.
Harold in Italy, op. 16. RCA Victor LSC 2228. [1958]
2s. 12 in. 33 1/3 rpm microgroove.
Symphony with viola solo
Boston Symphony Orchestra; William Primrose, viola;
Charles Munch, conductor.
Program notes by John N. Bulk on slipcase.
1. Symphonies. 2. Viola with orchestra.
I. Boston Symphony Orchestra. II. Primrose, William,
1904- III. Munch, Charles, 1891- IV. Title.

Uniform title is original French conventional title.

W. C. Fields; the original voice tracks from his greatest movies.
[Phonodisc] Decca DL 79164. [1968]
2s. 12 in. 33 1/3 rpm microgroove. Stereophonic.
With narration by Gary Owens and music composed and conducted
by Charles (Bub) Dant.
Playable also on monaural equipment.
Poster photo inserted in slipcase.
I. Fields, W. C., 1879-1946, II. Owen, Gary. III. Dant,
Charles.

Note lack of subject headings and entry under label title as main entry.
Performers names and date of phonorecording obtained by research of
item.

The Language and Music of the Wolves.
[Phonodisc] Columbia C 30769 [1971]
2s. 12 in. 33 1/3 rpm. microgroove. Stereophonic
Narrated by Robert Redford.
Notes by Charles Burr on Slipcase.
Contains Sounds of the Wolf, and The Wolf You Never Knew, by
Ron Holland
The Wolf You Never Knew, by Ron Holland
1. Wolves. 2. Animal sounds.
I. Redford, Robert. II. Holland, Ron.

Entry under jacket title. Note difference in producer and contents
note.

Brahms, Johannes, 1833-1897
[Quarter, strings, no. 1, op. 51, no. 1, C minor] Phonodisc.
String quartet no. 1, in C minor, op. 51, no. 1 Westminster
W 9019. [1963]
1 1/2 s. 12 in. 33 1/3 rpm. microgroove (collectors series)
Amadeus String Quartet.
Previously issued under serial no.: 18440
Duration: 29 min. 47 sec.
Program notes by Irving Kolodin on slipcase
With: Schubert, F.P. Quartet, strings, D 703, C minor.
1. String quartets.
I. Amadeus String Quartet.

Note difference in contents notes and lack of entry for Schubert
quartets, separate catalog entry.

Tiny Tim's 2nd Album. [Phonodisc]
Reprise Records RS 6323 [1968].
2s. 12 in. 33 1/3 rpm. microgroove. Stereophonic.
Popular songs: Tiny Tim with orchestra.
1. Music, Popular (Songs etc.) - U.S.
I. Tiny Tim.

Note difference in subject heading from information in the entry.

Strauss, Richard, 1864-1949
[Salome. Ah   Du wolltest mich dein Mund küssen lassen,
Jochanaan] Phonodisc.
Salome: Final scene. Columbia ML 2048. [1959]
1s. 10 in. 33 1/3 rpm. microgroove (Columbia masterworks)
Ljuba Welitsch, soprano; Metropolitan Opera Orchestra;
Fritz Reiner, conductor.
Sung in German
Program notes in slipcase.
With Chaikovskii, P.I. Eugene Onegin Letter scene.
1. Operas - Excerpts. I. Welitsch, Ljuba. II. New York.
Metropolitan Opera. Orchestra. III. Reiner, Fritz, 1888-
IV. Title.

Note difference between uniform title and label title. Library of
Congress practice of putting performers names in notes and then
making added entries with (or without) dates is clear. A separate
entry is made for the flip side.

Chaikovskii, Petr Ilich, 1840-1893.
[Eugene Oniegin. Letter scene] Phonodisc.
Eugene Oniegin; Op. 24: Tatiana's letter scene. Words by
Pushkin. Columbia ML 2048 [1949]
1s. 10 in. 33 1/3 rpm. microgroove (Columbia masterworks)
Ljuba Welitsch, soprano; Philharmonia Orchestra; Walter
Susskind, conductor
Sung in German
Program notes on slipcase
With: Strauss, Richard. Salome. Ach, du woltest mich dein
Mund küssen lassen, Jochanaan
1. Operas - Excerpts. I. Welitsch, Ljuba. II. Philharmonia
Orchestra. London. III. Susskind, Walter, 1913- IV. Title:
Tatiana's letter scene.

Note spelling of Tchaikovsky's name (unique in the Library of Congress).

Puccini, Giacomo, 1858-1924
[Tosca. Italian] Phonodisc
Tosca [opera in 3 acts] Words by Illica and Giacosca. Angel
3508 B/L [1953]
4s. 12 in. 33 1/3 rpm. microgroove.
Maria Menenghini Callas, soprano; Giuseppe di Stefano, tenor;
Tito Gobbi, baritone; supporting soloists; orchestra and chorus
of Teatro alla Scala, Milan; Victor de Sabota, conductor
Automatic sequence
Notes on the opera by Louis Biancolli, synopsis, and libretto
with English translation (19 p. illus) laid in container.
1. Operas. I. Callas, Maria, 1923- II. Stefano, Giuseppe
di, 1927- III. Gobbi, Tito. IV. Sabota, Victor de, 1892-
1967. V. Milan. La Scala. VI. Puccini, Giacomo, 1858-
1924. Tosca. Libretto. English and Italian. VII. Title.

Note that no entries are made for the librettists.

Ponchielli, Amilcare, 1834-1886.
[La Gioconda. Italian] Phonodisc
La Gioconda. [Complete recording] London A 4331 (5347-
5349) [1957]
6s. 12 in. 33 1/3 rpm. microgroove.
Starring Anita Cerquetti, Giulietta Simoniato, Mario del Monaco,
Ettore Bastianini, and Cesare Siepi, with orchestra and Coro of
the Maggio musicale fiorentino; Gianandrea Gavazzeni,
conductor
Automatic sequence
Program notes by Robert Boas on container; libretto, with
English translation (66 p.) laid in.
1. Operas. I. Cerquetti, Anita. II. Simoniato, Giulietta.
III. Monaco, Mario del. IV. Bastianini, Ettore. V. Siepi,
Cesare. VI. Florence. Maggio musicale fiorentino Coro.
VII. Florence. Maggio musicale fiorentino. Orchestra.
VIII. Gavazzeni, Gianandrea, 1909- IX. Ponchielli, Amilcare,
1834-1886. La Gioconda. Libretto. English and Italian.
X. Title.

Note that librettist has been omitted completely; also note the entries
for Maggio musicale Fiorentino.

Beethoven, Ludwig van, 1770-1827.
[Quartet, string, no. 10, op. 74 E flat major] Phonodisc.
String quartet in E flat major, op. 74. String quartet in F
minor, op. 95. Music Guild MS 863 [1970]

2s. 12 in. 33 1/3 rpm. microgroove. stereophonic.
Allegri String Quartet
Program notes by Irving Kolodin on slipcase
1. String quartets. I. Beethoven, Ludwig van, 1770-1827.
Quartets, String, no. 11, op. 95, F minor. Phonodisc 1970.
II. Allegri String Quartet.

Generally two works by the same composer are included in one entry
under the composer and the uniform title of the first work. Users
find this confusing. In these examples entries for performers are
made, although they may be omitted in some cases which seem to fit
no consistent pattern. The inclusion of the date of the phonorecording
is easy for the Library of Congress, which has access to copyright
records. The date would be a major stumbling block for catalogers
in other libraries.

Chapter 9

EXAMPLES OF UNIT ENTRIES

All the examples used in the book are shown with full, and at times, variant acceptable cataloging first for a library requiring access to performers, conventional titles, and individual works. The cards that would be duplicated for each of these entries is not shown.

Following this list is a second list of all the examples with brief-form cataloging showing only the most significant parts of the phonorecording. If the composer is shown, then the uniform title and/or conventional title is shown. Performers are omitted. If the performer is the most significant element, the appropriate name would be placed first. In some cases, the important identifying feature is the label title or jacket title of the phonorecording.

UNIT ENTRIES

Animal sounds "The Language and Music of the Wolves."
Tonsil Records, New York, N.Y.
003.
12" LPS

Field Nine

Contents:- Side 1: "The wolf you never knew," by Ron Holland. perf. by Robert Redford, Narrator. Side 2, "Sounds of the wolf."

Computer System Entries

1. Wolves.

Note that access to author and narrator is assured because Field Nine is searchable.

Ballet "Parade," by Erik Satie.
Perf. by Efrem Kurtz cond. Houston Symphony Orchestra.
Columbia ML 2019
10" LPM
With Ballet Suite "Les Matelots (The Sailors)," by George Auric

Computer system entries in Field Ten.

1. Orchestra

Ballet Suite "Les Matelots (The Sailors)," by George Auric.
Perf. by Efrem Kurtz cond. Houston Symphony Orchestra.
Columbia ML 2019
10" LPM
With Ballet "Parade," by Erik Satie.

Computer

1. Orchestra

Comic monologues, "W. C. Fields, The original voice tracks from
his greatest movies." Perf. by W. C. Fields. Decca DL 79164.
12" LPS

1. Fields, William Claude, Comedian.

Computer entry necessary for established form of names.

Comic Songs "That Was The Year That Was," by Tom Lehrer.
Perf. by the composer. Reprise RS 6179.
12" LPS
Contents:- National Brotherhood Week. - MLF Lullaby. -
George Murphy. - The Folk Song Army. - Smut. - Send the
Marines. - Pollution. - So Long Mom. - Whatever became of
Hubert. - New Math. - Alma. - Who's Next. - Wernher von
Braun. - The Vatican Rag.

Computer

1. Male Vocalist.

Composition for piano "Four Excursions," by Samuel Barber.
Perf. by Rudolf Firkusny, Piano: Columbia ML 2174.
10" LPM
With Symphonic work for soprano and orchestra
"Knoxville Summer of 1910," by Samuel Barber.

Computer

1. Piano.

Composition for piano "Moment Musical," in F minor, Op. 94,
no. 5, by Franz Schubert. Perf. by Ernest Groschel, Piano.
Cassette Music Corporation 8S525.
Program 1, part 1, Cartridge Stereo
With Symphony in C, no. 6, D 589 "Little C Major."

Manual system

    1. Schubert, Franz, 1797-1828. 2. Groschel, Ernest, Piano.
    3. "Moment Musical", no. 5. 4. Piano.

Compositions "I Like Tchaikovsky," by Peter Ilyitch Tchaikovsky.
Perf. by Carmen Dragon cond. The Capitol Symphony Orchestra;
Hollywood Bowl Symphony Orchestra. Capitol P-8617.
12" LPM
Contents: Side 1. Eugene Onegin, Polonaise. - "Nutcracker
Suite, Arabian Dance. - Chinese Dance." Cantabile. -
"Serenade for strings, Waltz." Side 2, Romance in F minor; -
Melodie; - Song "None but the Lonely Hear," Arr. by Carmen
Dragon. - "Capriccio Italien, Finale."

Computer

    1. Orchestra.

Concerto for cello, piano, and violin in C, Op. 56, "Triple,"
by Ludwig van Beethoven. Perf. by John Corigliano, Violin;
Leonard Rose, Cello; Walter Hendl, Piano; Bruno Walter cond.
New York Philharmonic. Columbia ML 2059.
10" LPM

Computer: Note order of instruments.

    1. Cello, Violin, and Piano & Orchestra.

Concerto for cello, piano, and violin in C, Op. 56 "Triple."
by Ludwig van Beethoven. Perf. by Sviatoslav Knushevitzky,
Cello; Lev Oborin, Piano; David Oistrakh, Violin; Malcolm
Sargent cond. The Philharmonia Orchestra. Angel S. 35697.
12" LPM

Computer

    1. Cello, Piano, Violin & Orchestra.

Concerto for clarinet in F minor, No. 1, Op. 73, by Carl Maria
von Weber. Perf. by David Glazer, Clarinet; Heilbronn Joerg
Faerber cond. Wuerttemberg Chamber Orchestra. Turnabout
TV 341515.

Bd 1, Side 1, 12" LPS
With Quintet for clarinet and strings in B flat, Op. 34.
Contents: Side 1, Bd. 2, Concertino for clarinet, Op. 26.
Robert Wagner cond. Innsbruck Symphony Orchestra.

Manual system entries.

1. Weber, Carl Maria von, 1786-1826. 2. Glazer, David,
Clarinet. 3. Faerber, Heilbronn Joerg, cond. Wuerttemberg
Chamber Orchestra. 4. Wagner, Robert, cond. Innsbruck
Symphony Orchestra. 5. Clarinet & Orchestra.

Concerto for piano in B flat, no. 2, Op. 19, by Ludwig van
Beethoven. Perf. by William Kapell, Piano; Vladimir
Golschmann cond. NBC Symphony Orchestra. RCA Victor LM 12
10" LPM.

Computer

1. Piano & Orchestra.

Concerto for piano in B flat, no. 2, Op. 83, by Johannes Brahms.
Perf. by Andre Watts, Piano; Leonard Bernstein cond. New
York Philharmonic. Columbia Masterworks MS 7134.
12" LPS

Computer

1. Piano & Orchestra.

Concerto for violin in A, no. 5, K. 219, by Wolfgang Amadeus
Mozart. Perf. by David Oistrakh, Violin, Franz Konwitschny
cond. Sachsische Staatskapelle Dresden. Deutsche Grammophon
Gesellschaft.
10" LPM

Computer

1. Violin & Orchestra.

Concerto for violin in D, no. 1, Op. 19, by Serge Prokofiev.
Perf. by Nathan Milstein, Violin; Carlo Maria Giulini cond.
The Philharmonia Orchestra. Angel 36009.
Side 1, 12" LPM
With Concerto for violin in G Minor, no. 2, Op. 63.

Computer

1. Violin & Orchestra.

Concerto for violin in D, no. 1, Op. 19, by Serge Prokofiev.
Perf. by Nathan Milstein, Violin; Carlo Maria Giulini cond.
The Philharmonia Orchestra. Angel 36009.
Side 1, 12" LPM

Field Eight

With Concerto for violin in G Minor, no. 2, Op. 63.

Computer

1. Violin & Orchestra.

Concerto for violin in D, Op. 61, by Ludwig van Beethoven.
Perf. by David Oistrakh, Violin; Sixten Ehrling cond.
Stockholm Festival Orchestra. Columbia 33 CX 1194.
12" LPM

Computer

1. Violin & Orchestra.

English dialects "Carolina Low-country Patois: Gullah in
Story and Rhyme." Perf. by Dick Reeves, Narrator.
Lenwal Enterprises 01080B.
12" LPM

Computer

1. Gullah (English dialect)

Etudes for piano, Op. 10, by Frederic Chopin. Perf. by
Guiomar Novaes, Piano. Vox PL 9070.
12" LPM
Contents: Side 2, Bd 4. Scherzo in B Minor, no. 1, Op. 10.

Computer

1. Piano.

Etudes for piano, Op. 25, by Frederic Chopin. Perf. by
Guiomar Novaes, Piano. Vox PL 7560.
12" LPM
Contents: Side 2, Bd 2: "Trois nouvelles etudes."

1. Piano. 2. "Trois nouvelles etudes." 3. Chopin,
Frederic, 1810-1849.

Manual system. Note sequence of entries, which depends on library
rules

Humor "The Bloopy Awards for Broadcasting's Classic Bloopers."
Kermit Schaefer Productions Kapp KS-3631.
12" LPS

Manual system

    1. Radio extracts.   2.   Television extracts.   3.   Humor.
    4.   Schaefer, Kermit, Producer.

Musical comedies - Selections "The Rodgers and Hart Song Book,"
by Richard Rodgers and Oscar Hammerstein.   Ella Fitzgerald,
Vocalist; Buddy Bregman cond. orchestra.   Verve MGV-4002-2.
4 sides 12" LPM
Contents: Side 1: Have you met Miss Jones? - You took advantage of me. - A ship without a sail. - To keep my love alive. -
Dancing on the ceiling. - The lady is a tramp. - With a song in
my heart. - Manhattan: Side 2: Johnny one note. - I wish I
were in love again. - Spring is here. - It never entered my mind.
- This can't be love. - Thou swell. - My romance. - Where or
when - Little girl blue: Side 3: Give it back to the Indians. -
Ten cents a dance. - There's a small hotel. - I didn't know
what time it was. - Everything I've got. - I could write a book.
- Blue room. - My funny valentine. Side 4: Bewitched. -
Mountain greenery. - Wait till you see her. - Lover. - Isn't it
romantic. - Here in my arms. - Blue moon. - My heart stood
still. - I've got five dollars.

Computer

    1.   Vocalist & Orchestra.

Musical comedy "My Fair Lady," by Frederic Loewe and Alan
Jay Lerner, arranged by Robert Russell Bennett and Phil Lang.
Perf. by Rex Harrison, Julie Andrews, Stanley Holloway,
Robert Coote, Philippa Bevans, Michael King, Vocalists;
Franz Allers, Musical Director.   Columbia Masterworks
OL 5090.
12" LPM

Manual system

    1.   Vocalists, Chorus, & Orchestra.   2.   Harrison, Rex,
Vocalist.   3.   Andrews, Julie, Vocalist.   3.   Holloway,
Stanley, Vocalist.   4.   Coote, Robert, Vocalist.   5.   Loewe,
Frederic.   6.   Lerner, Alan Jay.   7.   Bennett, Robert Russell.
8.   Lang, Phil.   9.   Allers, Franz, cond.

Musical comedy "Out of this World," by Cole Porter.
Perf. by Charlotte Greenwood, Priscilla Gillette, William
Redfield, Barbara Ashley, George Jongeyand, Vocalists;
Pembroke Davenport, Conductor.
Columbia Masterworks OL 4390.
12" LPM

Computer

    1. Vocalists, chorus & orchestra. (Optional)

Opera "Il Trovatore,P by Giuseppe Verdi. Perf. by Zinka
Milanov, Soprano; Fedora Barbieri, Mezzo Soprano; Jussi
Bjoerling, Tenor; Leonard Warren, Baritone; Robert Shaw
cond. Robert Shaw Chorale; Renato Cellini cond. RCA Victor
Orchestra. RCA Victor LM 6008.
2 side 12" LPM
Sung in Italian.

Computer: Librettist has been omitted.

Opera "La Gioconda," by Amilcare Ponchielli. Perf. by
Anita Cerquetti, Soprano; Franco Sacchi, Contralto; Mario
del Monaco, Tenor; Cesare Siepi, Bass; Giulietta Simoniato,
Mezzo Soprano; Ettore Bastianini, Bass; Gianandrea
Gavazzeni cond. Chorus and Orchestra of Maggio Musicale
Fiorentino. London LOR 90004.
4 sides; 2 7" reels 7.5 ips Stereo

Computer

    1. Solo Voices, Chorus, & Orchestra (Optional)

Opera "Tosca," by Giacomo Puccini. Perf. Maria Meneghini
Callas, Soprano; Giuseppe di Stefano, Tenor; Tito Gobbi,
Baritone; Franco Calabrese, Bass; Victor de Sabata cond.
Chorus and Orchestra of La Scala Opera House, Milan.
Columbia, 33CX1094.
4 sides 12" LPM
Sung in Italian.

Computer

    1. Solo Voices, Chorus & Orchestra. (Optional)

Opera "Tristan and Isolde," by Richard Wagner. Perf. by
Kirsten Flagstad, Soprano; Rudolf Schock, Tenor; Blanche
Thebom, Mezzo Soprano; Dietrich Fischer-Dieskau, Baritone;

Ludwig Suthaus, Tenor; Wilhelm Furtwaengler cond. The
Philharmonia Orchestra. RCA Victor Red Seal LM 6700.
10 sides 12" LPM
Sung in German.

Computer: (Optional Subject heading omitted)

Opera - Selections "Eugene Onegin, Tatiana's Letter Scene,"
by Peter Ilyitch Tchaikovsky. Perf. by Ljuba Welitsch, Soprano;
Walter Susskind cond. The Philharmonia Orchestra. Columbia
Masterworks ML 2048.
Side 2, 10" LPM
With Opera - Selections "Salome," Final Scene, by Richard
Strauss.

Computer

1. Soprano & Orchestra. (Subject heading mandatory)

Opera - Selections "Salome," Final Scene, by Richard Strauss.
Perf. by Ljuba Welitsch, Soprano; Fritz Reiner cond.
Metropolitan Opera Orchestra. Columbia Masterworks ML
2048. Side 1, 10" LPM
With Opera - Selections "Eugene Onegin," Tatiana's Letter Scene,
by Peter Ilyitch Tchaikovsky.

Computer

1. Soprano & Orchestra.

Operatic arias "Ten Tenors, Ten Arias." RCA Victor LM 1202.
12" LPM
Jacket title.
Contents: Side 1: "Il Trovatore, Di quella pira," by Verdi,
perf. by Beniamino Gigli, Tenor. - "Die Meistersinger,
Preislied," by Wagner, perf. by Set Svanholm, Tenor. -
"Faust, Salut demeure," by Gounod, perf. by Jussi Bjoerling. -
"Don Giovanni, Il mio tesoro," by Mozart, perf. by John
McCormack, Tenor. - "I Pagliacci, Vesti la giubba," by
Leoncavallo, perf. by Enrico Caruso, Tenor;   Side 2:
"L'Elisir D'Amore, Una furtiva lagrima," by Donizetti, perf.
by Ferrucio Tagliavini. - "La Boheme, Che gelida manina,"
by Puccini, perf. by Mario Lanza. - "Carmen, La fleur que tu
m'avais jetee," by Bizet, perf. by James Melton. - "Tosca,
E lucevan le stelle," by Puccini, perf. by Giuseppe di Stefano.

Computer

1. Tenor & Orchestra. 2. "Ten Tenors, Ten Arias."

Operatic arias "Verdi Rarities," by Giuseppe Verdi. Perf. by
Monserrat Caballe, Soprano, Anton Guadagno cond. RCA
Italian Opera Orchestra and Chorus. RCA Victor Red Seal
LSC 2995. 12" LPS
Contents: Side 1: "Un Giorno di Regno (Il Finto Stanislao):
Ah non m'hanno ingannato." - "I Lombardi: Qual prodigio
Non fu sogno " - "I Due Foscari: No, mi lasciate; tu al cui
sgardo onnipossente." - "Alzira: Riposa, tutte, in suo dolor
vegliante da Gusman ...": Side 2; "Attila: Liberamente or
piangi ..." - "Il Corsaro: Egli non riede ancora ..." -
"Aroldo: Oh, cielo Dove son'io ..."

Manual system

1. Caballe, Monserrat, Soprano. 2. Guadagno, Anton, cond.
RCA Italiana Opera Orchestra and Chorus. 3. Soprano, Chorus
& Orchestra. 4. Verdi, Giuseppe, 1813-1901.

Another order of elements in access field, Field Ten.

Overtures, "Four Overtures," by Hector Berlioz. Perf. by Jean
Martinon cond. L'Orchestre de L'Association des Concerts
Lamoureux. Urania UR-7048.
12" LPM
Contents: Side 1, The Corsair, Op. 21. - The Roman Carnival,
Op. 9. Side 2, King Lear, Op. 4 - Beatrice and Benedict.

Computer

1. Orchestra.

Poetry "Jean Cocteau Reads his Poetry and Prose."
Perf. by author. Caedmon TC 1083.
12" LPM
Contents: Side 1 Les voleurs d'enfants. - Plain-chant. -
L'ange heurtebise. - Hommage a Manolete. - Un ami mort.
Side 2: Les discours du Sphinx. - De l'innocence criminelle. -
De la responsibilite. - Le paquet rouge.

Computer

1. French language.

Popular music "Whipped Cream & Other Delights."
Perf. by Herb Alpert's Tijuana Brass. AM Records LP 110.
12" LPM
Contents: "A taste of honey." - "Green peppers." - "Tangerine."
- "Bittersweet samba." - "Lemon tree." - "Whipped cream."
- "Love potion 9." - "El garabanzo." - "Ladyfingers." -
"Butterball." - "Peanuts." - "Lollipops and roses."

Computer

    1. Dance band.

Popular songs "Pat Boone." Perf. by Pat Boone, Vocalist with
orchestra. Dot DLP 3012.
12" LPM
Contents:- Side 1, "Ain't that a shame." - "Rich in love." -
"Two hearts." - "No other arms." "Now I know." - "Gee
Whittakers." - "At my front door." - "Take the time." -
"Tutti frutti." - "Tra-la-la." - "Tennessee Saturday night." -
"I'll be home."

Computer

    1. Male Vocalist & Orchestra.

Popular songs "Pat's Great Hits, Vol. 2." Perf. by Pat Boone,
Vocalist; Billy Vaughn, cond. Dot DLP 3261.
12" LPM
Contents: Side 1: "A wonderful time up there." - "If dreams
come true." - "For my good fortune." - "Cherie, I love you."
- "When the swallows come back to Capistrano." - "Sugar moon."
- "It's too soon to know." - "April Love. " - "Gee, but it's
lonely." - "That's how much I love you." - "The Mardi Gras
march." - "I'll remember tonight."

Manual system

    1. Boone, Pat, Vocalist. 2. Vaughn, Billy, Cond.
    3. Male Vocalist & Orchestra.

Popular Songs "Tiny Tim's 2nd Album." Perf. by Tiny Tim
(Herbert Khaury) Vocalist. Reprise RS 6323.
12" LPS
Contents: "Come to the ball." - "My dreams are getting better
all the time." - "We love it." - "When I walk with you." -
"Community." - "She's just laughing at me." - "Have you seen
my little Sue?" - "Christopher Brady's ole lady." - "Great balls
of fire." - "Neighbourhood children." - "I can't help but wonder
where I'm bound." - "It's all right now." - "Down Virginia way."
- "Medley: I'm glad I'm a girl." - "I'm glad I'm a boy." -
"My hero." - "As time goes by."

Computer

    1. Male Vocalist & Orchestra.

Quartet for strings in C Minor, no. 1, Op. 51, no. 1, by
  Johannes Brahms, Perf. by Budapest String Quartet,
  Columbia ML 2191.
  10" LPM

Computer

  1. String Quartet

Quartet for strings in E flat, no. 10, Op. 74, "Harp," by
  Ludwig van Beethoven. Perf. by Fine Arts Quartet.
  Concert-Disc CS-257-A.
  Side 1, 12" LPM (Connoisseur Series)
  With Quartet for strings in F minor, no. 11, Op. 95, "Serioso."

Computer

  1. String Quartet.

Quartet for strings in F Minor, no. 11, Op. 95, "Serioso," by
  Ludwig van Beethoven. Perf. by Fine Arts Quartet.
  Concert-Disc CS-257.
  Side 2, 12" LPM (Connnoisseur Series)
  With Quartet for strings in E flat, no. 10, Op. 74, "Harp."

Computer

  1. String Quartet.

Quintet for clarinet and strings in B flat, Op. 34, by Carl Maria
  von Weber. Perf. by David Glazer, Clarinet; Kohon Quartet.
  Turnabout TV 341515.
  Side 2, 12" LPS.
  With Concerto for clarinet in F Minor, no. 1, Op. 73.

Manual System

  1. Weber, Carl Maria von, 1786-1826. 2. Glazer, David,
  Clarinet. 3. Kohon Quartet. 4. Clarinet & Strings.

Serenade "Italian," by Hugo Wolf. Perf. by William Steinberg
  cond. Pittsburgh Symphony Orchestra. Pickwick SPC-4027.
  Side 2, Bd. 1.
  Label title "Italian Style." By arrangement with Capitol Records.
  With Symphony in A, Op. 90, "Italian," by Felix Mendelssohn.
  Contents:- Side 2, Bd 2, Capriccio "Italien," by Peter Ilyitch
  Tchaikovsky.

Manual system

    1. Wolf, Hugo, 1860-1903. 2. Orchestra. 3. Steinberg, William, cond. Pittsburgh Symphony. 4. Pittsburgh Symphony cond. by William Steinberg.

Preferred arrangement of Field Ten: Composer, Subject heading, Performers

    Septet for piano, trumpet and strings, Op. 65, by Camille Saint-Saens. Perf. by Menahem Pressler, Piano; Harry Glantz, Trumpet; Philip Sklar, Bass; Guilet String Quartet. Heliodor H25012.
    12" LPM
    With Suite "In the Olden Style," by Vincent D'Indy.

Manual system

    1. Saint-Saens, Camille, 1835-1921. 2. Pressler, Menahem, Piano. 3. Glantz, Harry, Trumpet. 4. Sklar, Philip, Bass. 5. Guilet String Quartet. 6. Piano, Trumpet, & Strings.

Arrangement of Field Ten: Composer, Performer, Subject heading

    Sonata for piano in C, no. 21, Op. 53, "Waldstein." by Ludwig van Beethoven. Perf. by Claudio Arrau, Piano. Columbia ML 2078.
    10" LPM

Computer

    1. Piano

    Songs "A Florence Foster   Jenkins   Recital   " Perf. by Florence Foster Jenkins; Cosme McMoon, Piano. RCA Victor Red Seal LRT 7000.
    10" LPM
    Contents: Side 1; "The Magic Flute, Queen of the night's aria," by Mozart. - "The musical snuff-box," by Liadoff. - "Like a bird." by McMoon. - "Lakme, Bell song," by Delibes. - "Serenata Mexicana," by McMoon. Side 2: "Pearl of Brazil, Charmant oiseau." by David. - "Biassy." by Pavlovich, after Bach. - "Die Fledermaus, Adele's laughing song," by Johann Strauss, Jr.
    1. McMoon, Cosme, 1897 - 2. Jenkins, Florence Foster, Soprano. 3. McMoon, Cosme, Piano. 4. Soprano & Piano. 5. Title anals.

Manual system with full cataloging for music research library omitting only entries for composers.

Sound Track "The Countess from Hong Kong," by Charles Chaplin.
Music arranged and cond. by Lambert Williamson. Decca
DL 1501.
12" LPM

Manual system

1. Orchestra. 2. Chaplin, Charles. 3. Williamson,
Lambert, cond.

Sound Track "Oklahoma " by Richard Rodgers and Oscar
Hammerstein. Perf. by Gordon MacRae, Gloria Grahame,
Gene Nelson, Charlotte Greenwood, James Whitemore, Shirley
Jones, Vocalists; Jay Blackton, Conductor. Capitol SAO-595.
12" LPM

Computer

1. Vocalist, Chorus, & Orchestra. 2. Musical Comedy.
(Added Uniform title.)

Suite "In the Olden Style," for trumpet, two flutes, and strings,
Op. 24, by Vincent D'Indy. Perf. by Julius Baker, Flute;
Claude Monteux, Flute; Harry Glantz, Trumpet; Guilet String
Quartet. Heliodor H25012.
Side 1, 12" LPM
With Septet for piano, trumpet, and strings, Op. 65, by
Camille Saint-Saens.

1. "In the Olden Style." 2. D'Indy, Vincent, 1851-1931. 3.
Baker, Julius, Flute. 4. Monteux, Claude, Flute. 5. Glantz,
Harry, Trumpet. 6. Flutes, Trumpet, & Strings.

Manual system: Arrangement of Field Ten: Conventional title, Composer, Performers, Subject Heading.

Symphony in A, No. 4, Op. 90, "Italian," by Felix Mendelssohn.
Perf. by William Steinberg cond. Pittsburgh Symphony Orchestra.
Pickwick SPC 4027.
Side 1, 12" LPS
Label title: "Italian style." By arrangement with Capitol
Records. With Italian Serenade, by Hugo Wolf.

1. Mendelssohn, Felix, 1809-1847. 2. Steinberg, William
cond. Pittsburgh Symphony. 3. Pittsburgh Symphony cond. by
William Steinberg. 4. "Italian".

Manual system: Arrangement of Field Ten: Composer, Performers, Subject Heading, Conventional Title.

Symphony in B Minor, no. 2, by Alexander Borodin. Perf. by
Kurt Sanderling cond. Saxon State Orchestra. Heliodor H25061.
Side 1, 12" LPM
With "In the Steppes of Central Asia."

Manual system

1. Borodin, Alexander, 1833-1887. 2. Sanderling, Kurt,
cond. Saxon State Orchestra. 3. Saxon State Orchestra cond.
by Kurt Sanderling. 4. Orchestra.

Symphony in C, no. 6, D 589, "Little," by Franz Schubert. Perf.
by Alexander Von Pitamic cond. Sueddeutsche Philharmonic
Orchestra. Cassette Music Corporation 8S525.
Program 1, concluded, 2, 3, & 4, Cartridge Stereo.
With Composition for piano "Moment Musical." in F minor.
Op. 9, no. 5.

Computer

1. Orchestra.

Symphony in C, no. 41, K 551, "Jupiter," by Wolfgang Amadeus
Mozart. Perf. by Bruno Walter cond. Columbia Symphony
Orchestra. Columbia MQ436.
Side 1, 7" reel 7.5 ips Stereo.
With Symphony in D, no. 35, K385 "Haffner."

Computer

1. Orchestra.

Symphony in D, no. 2, Op. 43, by Jean Sibelius. Perf. by
Leopold Stokowski cond. members of the NBC Symphony
Orchestra. RCA Victor LM 1854.
12" LPM

Computer

1. Orchestra

Symphony in D, no. 2, Op. 43, by Jean Sibelius. Perf. by
Sir John Barbirolli cond. The Halle Orchestra. Angel
Y1S-35425.
7" Reel 3.75 ips Stereo
Contents:- Side 2, Bd 2, Symphonic work "Lemminkainen
Legend," - Selection "The Swan of Tuonela." Op. 22, no. 3.

Computer

1. Orchestra.

Symphony in E flat, no. 5, Op. 82, by Jean Sibelius. Perf. by
Herbert von Karajan cond. The Philharmonia Orchestra.
Angel 35922.
12" LPM
Contents: Side 2, Bd 2, Symphonic poem "Finlandia," Op. 26.

Computer

    1. Orchestra.

Symphony in G, no. 94, "Surprise," by Franz Joseph Haydn.
Perf. by Norddeutscher Rundfunk-Orchester, Hamburg. Vox
PL 12.510.
Side 1, 12" LPM
With Symphony in C, no. 41, K. 551. "Jupiter," by Wolfgang
Amadeus Mozart.

Computer

    1. Orchestra.

Symphonic work "Das Lied von der Erde," by Gustav Mahler.
Perf. by Elsa Cavelti, Mezzo Soprano; Anton Dermota, Tenor;
Otto Klemperer cond. Vienna Symphony. Vox PL 7000.
12" LPM.

Computer

    1. Mezzo Soprano, Tenor & Orchestra.

Symphonic work "Harold in Italy," Op. 16, by Hector Berlioz.
Charles Munch cond. Boston Symphony Orchestra; William
Primrose, Viola. RCA Victor LSC-2228.
12" LPS

Computer

    1. Viola & Orchestra.

Symphonic work "In the Steppes of Central Asia," by Alexander
Borodin. Perf. by Kurt Sanderling cond. Saxon State
Orchestra. Heliodor H25061.
Bd 1, Side 2, 12" LPM
With Symphony in B minor, no. 2.
Contents:- Side 1, Bd 2, Symphonic poem "Romeo and Juliet,"
by Peter Ilyitch Tchaikovsky.

Manual system

    1. Borodin, Alexander. 2. "In the Steppes of Central Asia."
    3. Sanderling, Kurt, cond. Saxon State Orchestra. 4. Saxon

State Orchestra cond. by Kurt Sanderling. 5. Orchestra. 6.
Composer, Title anals.

Information from Field Nine to be used as entries.

Symphonic work "Royal Fireworks Music," by George Frederic
Handel. Perf. by Fritz Lehman cond. Berlin Philharmonic
Orchestra, Archive Production. APM 16031
10" LPM

Computer

    1. Orchestra.

Symphonic work for soprano and orchestra "Knoxville Summer of
1915," by Samuel Barber. Text by James Agee. Perf. by
Eleanor Steber, Soprano; William Strickland cond. Dumbarton
Oaks Chamber Orchestra. Columbia ML2174.
10" LPM
With composition for piano "Four Excursions."

Computer

    1. Soprano & Orchestra.

Waltzes "Waltz " Perf. by Carmen Dragon cond. Hollywood Bowl
Symphony Orchestra. Capitol Symphony Orchestra. Capitol
SP-8623.
12" LPS
Contents: Side 1: Waltz in E flat, Op. 18, "Grande Valse
Brilliante," by Chopin. - Waltz "La Plus que Lente," by
Debussy. - Waltz from "Coppelia." by Delibes. - Waltz in A flat,
Op. 39, no. 15, by Brahms. - Waltz "Musetta's Waltz Song,"
from "La Boheme," by Puccini: Side 2: Waltz from "Faust,"
by Gounod. - Waltz "Valse Triste," Op. 44, by Sibelius. -
Waltz in D flat, Op. 64, no. 1, "Minute Waltz," by Chopin. -
Waltzes from "The Gypsy Baron," by Johann Strauss, Jr.

Computer

    1. Orchestra.

BRIEF-FORM CATALOG

Alpert (Herb) Tijuana Brass: "Whipped Cream and Other Delights."
AM Records 110.

Auric: "The Sailors (Les Matelots)" Columbia 2019.

Barber: "Four Excursions," Columbia 2174.

Barber: "Knoxville, Summer of 1915." Columbia 2174.

Beethoven: Piano concerto no. 2. RCA Victor. 12.

Beethoven: Quartet for strings, no. 10, "Harp." Concert-Disc 257.

Beethoven: Quartet for strings, no. 11, "Serioso." Concert-Disc 257.

Beethoven: Sonata for piano, no. 21, "Waldstein." Columbia 2078.

Beethoven: "Triple" concerto for cello, violin, and piano. Angel 35697.

Beethoven: "Triple" concerto for cello, violin, and piano. Columbia 2059.

Beethoven: Violin concerto. Columbia 1194.

Berlioz: "Four Overtures." Urania 7048.

Berlioz: "Harold in Italy." RCA Victor 2228.

"The Bloopy Awards for Broadcasting's Classic Bloopers." Kapp 3631.

Boone (Pat). Dot 3012.

Boone (Pat): "Pat's Great Hits, Vol. 2." Dot 3261.

Borodin: "In the Steppes of Central Asia." Heliodor 25061.

Borodin: Symphony no. 2. Heliodor 25061.

Brahms: Quartet for strings, no. 1. Columbia 2191.

Brahms: Piano concerto no. 2. Columbia 7134.

Caballe (Monserrat): "Verdi Rarities." RCA Victor 2995.

Chaplin (Charles): "The Countess from Hong Kong." Sound track. Decca 1501.

Chopin: Etudes for piano, Op. 10. Vox 9070.

Chopin: Etudes for piano, Op. 25. Vox 7560.

Cocteau (Jean): "...Reads his Poetry and Prose." Caedmon 1083.

D'Indy: Suite "In the Olden Style," for trumpet, two flutes, and strings. Heliodor 25012.

Fields (W. C.): "...Voice Tracks from His Greatest Movies." Decca 79164.

Fitzgerald (Ella): "The Rodgers and Hart Song Book." Verve 4002.

"Gullah in Story and Rhyme: Carolina Lowcountry Patois." Lenwal
   Enterprises 01080.

Handel: "Royal Fireworks Music." Archive 16031.

Haydn: Symphony no. 94, "Surprise." Vox 12.510.

Jenkins (Florence Foster): "A Florence Foster Jenkins Recital."
   RCA Victor 7000.

"Language and Music of the Wolves," Tonsil Records 003.

Lehrer (Tom): "That Was The Year That Was." Reprise 6179.

Mahler: "Das Lied von der Erde." Vox 7000.

Mendelssohn: Symphony no. 4, "Italian." Pickwick 4027.

Mozart: Symphony no. 41, "Jupiter." Columbia 436.

Mozart: Violin concerto no. 5. DGM 16101.

"My Fair Lady." Original cast. Columbia 5090.

"Oklahoma." Sound track. Capitol 595.

"Out of this World." Original cast. Columbia 4390.

Ponchielli: "La Gioconda." London 90004. Reel.

Prokofiev: Violin concerto no. 1. Angel 36009.

Puccini: "Tosca." Columbia 1094.

Saint-Saens: Septet for piano, trumpet and strings. Heliodor 25012.

Satie: "Parade." Columbia 2019.

Schubert: "Moment Musical," F minor, Op. 95, no. 5. Cassette
   Music Corp. 8S525. Cartridge.

Schubert: Symphony no. 6, "Little C Major." Cassette Music
   Corp. 8S525. Cartridge.

Sibelius: Symphony no. 2. Angel 35425.

Sibelius: Symphony no. 2. RCA Victor 1854.

Sibelius: Symphony no. 5. Angel 35922.

Strauss: "Salome, Final Scene." Columbia 2048.

Tchaikovsky: "Evgen Onegin, Tatiana's Letter Scene." Columbia
   2048.

Tchaikovsky: Selections "I Like Tchaikovsky." Capitol 8617.

"Ten Tenors, Ten Arias." RCA Victor 1202.

Tiny Tim (Herbert Khaury): "Tiny Tim's 2nd Album." Reprise 6323.

Verdi: "Il Trovatore." RCA Victor 6008.

Wagner: "Tristan and Isolde." RCA Victor 6700.

"Waltz " Carmen Dragon, symphony orchestra. Capitol 8623.

Weber, Carl Maria von: Clarinet concerto, no. 1, Turnabout 341515.

Weber, Carl Maria von: Quintet for clarinet and strings. Turnabout 341515.

Wolf (Hugo): "Italian Serenade." Pickwick 4027.

Entries may be made under conventional title or performer or composer, whichever is the unifying element. The title of musical comedies, the performers of popular music, and the composers of serious music for orchestra - with or without soloists - is generally the unifying element. Titles are put in quotes and the first name of performers is included in parenthesis. Where conflict might arise, the first name of composers is given. It may be omitted if no conflict would arise as indicated in Schwann Record and Tape Guide.

INDEX OF PHONORECORDINGS
USED AS EXAMPLES IN CHAPTERS 3-8

SUBJECT INDEX

A

Access fields, 6, 113-138
Added entries, 18, 124
Additional description, 17,
104-105, 110, 115-116
Aeneid, 14
Anglo-American Cataloging
Rules, 1967, 3, 30, 67,
139-141
Animal sounds, 30-32, 45, 137
Arrangers, 50, 62
Authors, 64
"Avalon" (popular song), 8

B

"Blue Moon" (popular song), 28
Boito, Arrigo, 17, 49
Brief form cataloging (Brief-
listing), 21, 27, 36, 47, 91,
164-167

C

Caedmon Records, 67
Cartridge phonotapes, 4-5,
98-101
Caruso, Enrico, 1
Cassette phonotapes, 5, 98-101
Collections (contents of phono-
recordings), 8, 22, 26, 116-120
Composer (author equivalent),
15, 49-64, 107-108
Computers; computerized
cataloging, 3, 13, 29, 68-69

Conductors, 70, 91
Contents (Field Nine), 17, 113-124
Conventional titles, 38-46
Cylinder phonorecording, 1

E

Edison, Thomas A., 1

F

Fields of information, 14-17, 20-32,
106-111
Foreign languages, 10, 76-78, 137

H

Harrison tape catalog, 3

I

Identifying numbers, 16, 102-103,
110-111
Instrumental groups, 80, 136-137

J

Jackets (phonodisc containers), 13,
35, 41, 86
Jazz, 9, 44
Jenkins, Florence Foster, 85-86,
130

L

Labels, 13-14, 20-32, 35, 72, 77
Libraries, 2, 9, 30, 33, 68, 101
Library of Congress, 3, 139-142

171

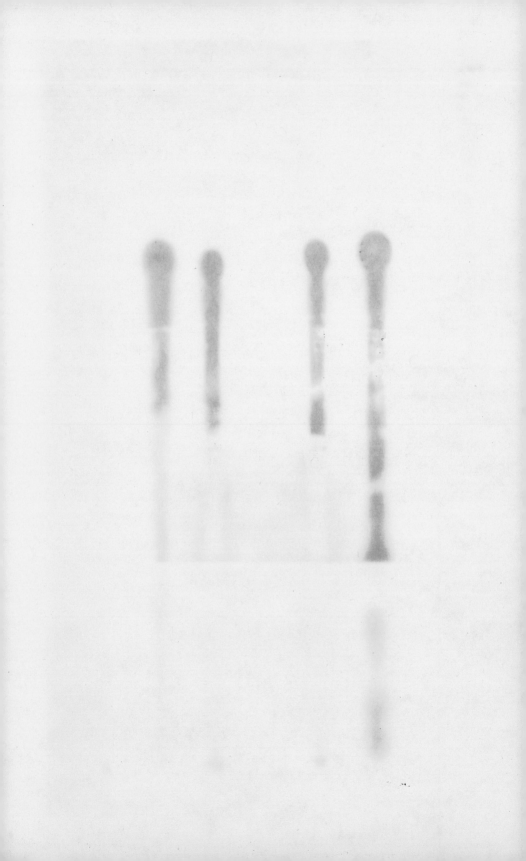